Italian Lakes
& Verona

Text by Susie Boulton
Edited by Anna Tyler
Series Editor: Tony Halliday

Berlitz® POCKET GUIDE

Italian Lakes
& Verona

First Edition 2007

PHOTOGRAPHY
By Anna Mockford and Nick Bonetti except: 63, 64, 65, 75, 77, 78, 79, 80, 87 Glyn Genin; 21, 87 George Taylor; 15, 20 AKG.
Cover photograph: Art Kowalsky/Alamy

CONTACTING THE EDITORS
Every effort has been made to provide accurate information in this publication, but changes are inevitable. The publisher cannot be responsible for any resulting loss, inconvenience or injury. We would appreciate it if readers would call our attention to any errors or outdated information by contacting Berlitz Publishing, PO Box 7910, London SE1 1WE, England.
Fax: (44) 20 7403 0290
Email: berlitz@apaguide.co.uk
<www.berlitzpublishing.com>

Bergamo's Città Alta (page 63) is packed with magnificent medieval and Renaissance monuments

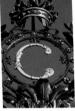

Villa Carlotta (page 42), famed for its sumptuous gardens, sits on Lake Como's western shore

Built in 1787 for an eccentric cardinal, Villa del Balbianello (page 40) embodies the effortless style and beauty of the region

TOP TEN ATTRACTIONS

With its 13th-century castle, Sirmione (page 47) is one of Lake Garda's most visited resorts

Bellagio (page 43), the 'pearl of Lake Como', enjoys unrivalled panoramic mountain views

Villa Taranto's botanical gardens (page 30) are planted with around 20,000 different species of trees, shrubs and flowers

Once the scene of gladiatorial combat, Verona's Roman Arena (page 76) stages operatic extravaganzas

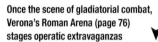

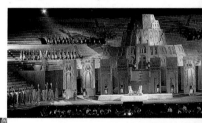

The picturesque fishing village of Malcesine (page 55) lies at the foot of Monte Baldo

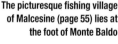

The church of Santa Caterina del Sasso (page 32) clings to a cliff face above Lake Maggiore

The Borromeo Islands (page 26) make a suitably grandiose home for an ostentation of peacocks

CONTENTS

A ➤ in the text denotes a highly recommended sight

Fact Sheets

INTRODUCTION

Set among the southern foothills of the Alps, the Italian lakes extend over four different regions of northwest Italy: Piedmont, Lombardy, Trentino and the Veneto. The famous trio are Maggiore, Como and Garda, but there are also a number of smaller, peaceful lakes scattered among the valleys.

Each lake has its own character, whether it is tiny, jewel-like Orta, with its perfectly preserved medieval village and islet; beguiling Como where mountains plunge into the deep waters and picture-postcard villages cling to the slopes; vast and varied Garda – fjord-like in the north, sea-like in the south; or stately Maggiore, where snowcapped mountains form a dramatic backdrop to the enchanting Borromeo islands. What they all have in common is a fertile shoreline, with a varied and exotic array of flora that thrives in the benign spring-to-autumn climate.

Villas, Gardens and Castles

Sumptuous lakeside villas and their gardens, created original-ly for northern European nobility or well-heeled Milanese, are a major draw of the larger lakes. Como in particular has drawn the rich and famous, from Pliny the Younger who built villas at Bellagio to George Clooney who recently purchased a lakeside villa at Laglio. Palatial residences such as Como's Villa d'Este and Villa Serbelloni have been converted to lux-ury hotels, other villas and gardens throw their gates open to the public, and those in private hands can be admired from the lake as you chug past on a ferryboat.

Incongruous with the mountain settings, the lake shores are Riviera-like, studded with olive groves, palms and citrus

A view across the rooftops of Stresa by Lake Maggiore

Sumptuous style at Villa Balbinello on Lake Como

trees; lakeside promenades are lined by palms and oleanders while throughout the spring a proliferation of azaleas, rhododendrons and camellias create a blaze of colour on the gently sloping banks.

Rising above the lakeshore villages are the lofty belltowers of Romanesque churches and the battlements of medieval castles. On Lake Garda the crenellated castles were the work of the power-hungry Scaligeri from Verona, on Maggiore the fortifications and island *palazzi* were built by the Borromeo family of Milan – who to this very day own the islands and the lake's main castle at Angera.

A Playground for the Rich and Famous

As with every beautiful corner of Italy, the region is steeped in association with famous figures. In Roman times the poet Catullus owned a villa at Sirmione, Virgil was born near Mantua and the writer/historians Pliny the Elder and Pliny the Younger came from Como. Shelley, Wordsworth and other romantic poets were bewitched by the dramatic natural beauty of the deep-blue waters and mountain peaks. Shelley sung the praises of Lake Como: 'it surpasses in beauty everything I have ever seen hitherto'.

In the late-19th century the lakes became a pleasure ground for the rich, royal and famous. Queen Victoria stayed in Villa Cara at Baveno near Stresa in 1879; later the Grand Hotel in Gardone Riviera on Lake Garda hosted Somerset Maugham, Vladimir Nabokov and Winston Churchill. D.H. Lawrence, in describing Limone on Lake Garda, wrote of 'a lake as beautiful as the beginning of creation'. Hemingway, who was recuperating after a battle wound at Stresa's Grand Hotel des Iles Borromées in 1918, used the resort as a back-drop in *A Farewell to Arms*.

The region also has a strong musical heritage and was a favourite haunt of famous composers. Montiverdi and violin-maker Antonio Stradivarius came from Cremona; Lake Como gave inspiration to Verdi, Rossini and Liszt.

Negotiating the Lakes

The main lakes see large numbers of holidaymakers from late spring to early autumn. Long stretches of the lakeside, including Como's eastern shore and much of Lake Maggiore's western one, are spoilt by heavy traffic on narrow and tortuous roads. While a car is clearly useful for touring, it is far more relaxing to base yourself in one lake resort and hop around by boat.

Ferries, hydrofoils and excursion cruisers provide excellent services linking almost all the towns and villages. Get up early and you can tour an entire lake, even one as big as Maggiore or Como, and have lunch on board the ferry. Cable cars, which climb to vantage points on the hillsides above the lakes, also offer some sensational views.

Historic Cities

The southern stretches of the region, typified by the flatlands of the Po and great swathes of industry, are also home to artistically rich cities such as Bergamo, Brescia, Mantua and Verona. In the heart of the cities (or in the case of Bergamo on top of the hill) there are fine historic centres bearing the marks of centuries of history. While Bergamo and Verona are immediately appealing, Mantua and Brescia are more of an acquired taste. Verona apart, these historic cities are comparatively free of crowds and commercialism, being bypassed by tourists making a beeline for Italy's more famous cities. Easily accessed from the lakes, they make ideal destinations for day trips.

Just an hour's drive from lakes Maggiore and Como, Milan is Italy's economic and cultural capital. Though famous for fashion, it has artistic riches too, among them the vast Gothic Duomo, Leonardo's *Last Supper* and the Brera art gallery.

Which Lake?

The main resorts on Maggiore and Como have a comfortable genteel charm, attracting large numbers of older visitors (mainly British and German) who are content to enjoy the scenery from the lakeside promenade, take boat trips around the lakes, visit islands, gardens and lakeside villas and take funicular rides to admire the views. On Lake Maggiore the grande dame resort of Stresa is the main place to stay, just a ferry hop from the Borromeo Islands. Upper Maggiore lies in Switzerland and although the resorts are Italian in feel, with their sunny piazzas and alfresco eateries, there is a marked Swiss efficiency

> The lakes are often referred to by their old Roman names: *Verbano* for Maggiore (after the verbena that flourished and still flourishes on its shores), *Lario* for Como, *Benaco* ('Beneficent') for Garda, *Cusio* for Lake Orta and *Sebino* for Lake Iseo.

Arriving at Bellagio on Lake Como

about them. Lake Como, particularly popular with the British and Americans, is the most romantic of the lakes, offering dramatic scenery, picturesque villages, belle époque resorts and the beautiful village of Bellagio at the heart of the lake.

German-orientated Lake Garda generally attracts a younger crowd, and is more suitable for families. There are sports, beaches and theme parks galore, and sufficient nightlife to keep the energetic entertained until the early hours. The lakes in general are a sporting paradise, offering watersports, hiking, mountain biking, skiing (in winter) and adventure sports. Lake Garda, with all those and more, is one big fitness centre. The *pelèr* (or *suer*) wind from the north, and the *ora* from the south, ensure superb sailing and windsurfing conditions, especially at the northern end of the lake. The mountains and ridges above the lakes offer endless opportunities for hikers and rock climbers; and for the less actively inclined there are cable cars up the slopes where you can enjoy some breathtaking views.

Then there is little Lake Orta, the only Italian lake lying entirely in Piedmont. The village of Orta San Giulio, overlooking the tiny Isola San Giulio, is arguably the most picturesque of any in the lakes and is certainly worthy of a detour from Lake Maggiore. Tranquil Lake Iseo, between lakes Como and Garda, is also pretty, surrounded by wooded mountains.

Escaping the Crowds

The lakes that once inspired the literati now provide a weekend or holiday retreat for Milanese industrialists, film stars and fashion designers. Add to these the spring-to-autumn package tours from Germany and the UK and it is not surprising that stretches of the lakeshores, particularly in southern Garda, have witnessed high-density development. The mountains and steep shores elsewhere, however, have precluded costa-like development and the backdrops remain largely rural. Even the most tourist-focused towns on the lakes have a picturesque medieval core of quiet cobbled alleys and a lakeshore terrace where you can linger over local wine and lake fish, watching steamers chug across the glassy waters. The lakes may not be the tranquil havens they once were, but the settings are as alluring as ever.

Enjoying a beach on Lake Garda

A BRIEF HISTORY

This region's remarkable landscape was formed at the end of the last Ice Age when the Alpine glaciers retreated, leaving deep lake-filled valleys. For over 10 thousand years people have also been leaving their mark here, from the pre-historic rock carvings at Val Camonica to the magnificent 17th- and 18th-century villas that surround Lake Como. The region's location on trade routes between Rome and central Europe played a crucial role in its history, ensuring prosperity, but also luring a succession of foreign invaders.

Early Settlers

Lombardy and the lakes lie within a larger area that the Romans called Gallia Cisalpina ('Gaul this side of the Alps'), a vast wild tract of land and lakes. Gallic tribes, pushing south from the Rhine Valley, were inhabiting the fertile plains of the Po Valley by the 4th century BC, creating their settlements at what are now Milan, Brescia, Verona, Mantua, Bergamo and Como. In 224BC the Romans put an end to these Celtic forays by conquering the area south of the Po, and a year later Flaminius crossed the river, dismantled its

The most conspicuous legacies of Roman rule are Brescia's Capitoline Temple (*see below*) and Roman theatre and Verona's superbly preserved arena, the third largest surviving from ancient times.

Roman mosaic in Villa Romana at Desenzano del Garda

bridges and defeated the Celtic tribes, including the powerful Insubres.

However, during the Second Punic War and its aftermath, when the Romans were more concerned with defeating Hannibal, the Gauls rose up again, attacking the Roman fortresses on the Po. Consular armies were despatched north, defeating the tribes at the River Mincio near Mantua. A further victory near Lake Como finally obliged the Gauls to sue for peace. With the final reduction of Cisalpine Gaul, the Celtic tribes were progressively merged with the Romans.

Huns, Goths and Lombards

By the 3rd century AD Cisalpine Gaul had become a commercially prosperous region of the Roman Empire and an important gateway to northern Europe. Attila the Hun, invading his way through Italy, plundered and pillaged Milan, Verona, Bergamo and Brescia in AD452, but after the mediation of Pope Leo I, the infamous barbarian warrior halted at the Po and promised never to return.

Following the breakdown of the Western Roman Empire in 476 the region was subject to further waves of invaders. The German Odoacer crowned himself king at Pavia but was later vanquished by Theodoric the Ostrogoth. During his 40-year reign Theodoric ruled through surviving Roman institutions, welding together Goths and Romans, administering justice, and creating fine buildings, including a palace for himself in Verona on the site of the present-day Castelvecchio.

The Lombards, a warfaring Germanic tribe, descended on the region in 568, putting an end to any vestige of political unity that may have survived the Roman era. They crossed the Alps in the spring of 568, and two years later they had conquered all the main cities north of the Po, with the exception of Pavia, seat of the royal palace. Their kingdom in Italy lasted a couple of centuries and was in the main ruled by the king and his royal officials who kept a check on the power of the dukes and counts. The Lombards were eventually absorbed into the Italian population, adopting Roman life and customs, freely intermarrying and, in many cases, converting to Christianity. Ethnically and socially they left an indelible mark on the people of northern Italy.

Invasion of papal territories by the Lombards forced the pope to appeal for support from Pepin, the Christian king of the Franks. In 774 Pepin's son Charlemagne and his army conquered much of Italy, including the north, and took the Lombard crown.

Charlemagne

On Christmas Day 800 Pope Leo III revived the Roman imperial title when he crowned Charlemagne Holy Roman Emperor. However, the Franks failed to establish a durable state in Italy and in 1024 the royal palace at Pavia, symbol of the power of the Holy Roman Empire, was destroyed by the local people.

Fresco depicting the Visconti family's capture of Milan in 1277

Era of the Communes

The early 11th century saw the emergence of the commune, or free city-state, the quintessential institution of medieval northern Italy. Prior to this, local aristocrats and the emerging commercial classes had been prepared to play second fiddle to the state in exchange for a degree of patronage from the emperor or king. As the rulers' power and influence waned, the strength and independence of the aristocrats and tradesmen increased.

As a consequence, economic and de facto governmental power passed to the localities, giving birth to the communes. These were self-governing municipal institutions with their origins in rebellion, treaty or charter. Typical rights included the control of justice, personal liberty of the townsmen and powers to regulate trade and levy local taxes and tolls. Milan acquired communal status in 1045, followed later by Brescia, Como, Bergamo, Verona and Mantua.

These communes were vulnerable to factional feuds, with powerful families often grouping together and gobbling up rival city-states. The great ideological conflict between the papacy and the Holy Roman Empire gave further impetus to conflict when these 'superpowers' vied for support in the northern cities. Within each city-state rival families adopted the labels 'Guelph' for the papacy and 'Ghibelline' for the empire. The famous vendetta in Verona between Montagues (Ghibellines) and Capulets (Guelphs) is just one example.

The Great Dynasties

The 13th century saw a shift in territorial and city-state power. The main cities fell to despotic rulers: Milan to the Visconti, Mantua to the Bonacolsi, Verona to the della Scalas (or Scaligeri). By the mid-14th century the smaller cities had lost their independent communal status. Milan had swallowed up great swathes of northern Italy and by 1402 had even extended its territories south to Tuscany.

As well as able administrators, the family dynasties were dynamic patrons of the arts. Milan and Mantua, which was by now under the civilizing rule of the Gonzagas, were great centres of art, drawing the leading artists, poets and scholars of the time. Under the mighty Visconti dynasty, cathedrals, fortresses and *palazzi* were constructed across the region, among them the cathedrals of Milan and Como and the Certosa (Charterhouse) of Pavia. Ludovico il Moro of the Sforza family,

The ruthless and tyrannical Scaligeri dynasty ruled Verona from 1260 to 1387. A number of their castles, all with characteristic fishtail battlements, can be seen around Lake Garda (Castello Scaligero at Malcesine is below) and their elaborate Gothic mausoleums still stand in central Verona (see page 78).

who inherited Milan from the Visconti, attracted Bramante, the great High Renaissance architect and decorative painter; and Leonardo da Vinci, who produced most of his ground-breaking artistic, scientific and medical studies here. The Mantuan court drew the great Florentine architect, Alberti, and the painter, Mantegna, who glorified the Gonzaga family in his brilliant fresco decorations. Verona produced the great Renaissance artist, Veronese, and celebrated architects such as Sanmicheli; Brescia produced its own school of painters; Bergamo played host to a whole range of painters from the workshops of Milan and Venice, and saw the creation of the Colleoni Chapel, a masterpiece of the Lombard Renaissance.

From the early 1400s the republic of Venice, until then an exclusively maritime power, with naval bases from the lagoon

Saint Carlo Borromeo (1538–84)

Born into the Borromeo dynasty (who to this day own the Borromeo islands, the castle at Angera and the fishing rights of the entire lake), the ascetic Carlo became a leading light in the Catholic Counter-Reformation. He was born in the (now ruined) castle of Arona on the southern shores of Lake Maggiore and devoted his life to the reform and welfare of the church. Appointed cardinal and Archbishop of Milan by his uncle, Pope Pius IV, Carlo founded seminaries and colleges for the education of clerical and lay members, rid Milan's Duomo of all its ornamentation, paid regular visits to hundreds of parishes and worked ceaselessly during the plague of 1576–8 to accommodate the sick and bury the dead. However, political turmoil beset him as he became embroiled in disputes with the governor and senate, and faced rebellion from various religious orders. In 1569 members of the order of the Humiliati (Brothers of Humility) hatched an unsuccessful conspiracy to take his life. Carlo was canonised posthumously by Pope Paul V in 1610.

to Constantinople, had begun to extend her net into the hinterland. Starting with Verona in 1405, huge swathes of territory were taken by military conquest from Milan, including Brescia and Bergamo, to extend the Venetian Empire to the River Adda. In 1454 the war was ended by the Peace of Lodi and an Italian league was formed, made up of the two dominant powers in the area, Milan and Venice, plus Florence.

Saint Carlo Borromeo, who was born in Arona

Foreign Intervention

In the late 15th and early 16th centuries, the small duchies that made up Italy became a battleground in the struggle between France and Habsburg Spain, the two great powers of the age. In the aftermath of the 1525 Battle of Pavia, when the French were expelled from the Duchy of Milan, treaties with the Pope settled the future of Italy for the next two centuries. The state of Milan was restored to the Sforza dynasty, but on the death of Francesco II in 1535 it fell under the domination of the Spanish Habsburg Emperor, Charles V, who later granted the duchy to his son, the future Philip II of Spain. Spanish rule was to endure until 1706. Venice on the other hand, with its increased territorial domains, maintained its independence. The Gonzaga rule of Mantua survived the territorial aggrandisements of both Milan and Venice, and the ruling family continued as masters of Mantua until the early 18th century.

In Spanish northern Italy the kaleidoscope of dynastic and interstate struggle gave way to a period of economic stagnation

The Battle of Solferino in 1859

and political decline. Executive power was in the hands of a governor, assisted by a senate, but important directives came from Madrid. The Italian aristocratic and bourgeois classes lost their political and commercial vigour and the effects were compounded by military levies and requisitions in support of Spanish wars, inflation, famine and plague.

During the War of Spanish Succession (1702–13) Austria seized control of most of northern Italy, including the Lakes. In 1796, following his victories in Piedmont, Napoleon swept into Lombardy and the northern cities became part of the short-lived Cisalpine Republic, allied with France. At the close of the Napoleonic wars Lombardy was restored to Austria, under the Congress of Vienna.

Austrian rule, which if anything was disliked even more than that of Spain, finally came to an end when Camillo Cavour, the architect of Italian unification, decided that the only way of defeating Austria was with the support of

France. In 1859 two thousand French troops were moved by rail into northern Italy under the command of Napoleon III. The Austrians were defeated first at Magenta, west of Milan, and then at Solferino, close to Lake Garda, this time with the help of Italian troops who either fought with the French or deserted the Austrian side. Some 40,000 men perished in the battle, inspiring the Swiss humanitarian, Henri Durant, who witnessed the carnage, to found the International Red Cross. The battles of Magenta and Solferino can be seen as a watershed in the military campaign for the unification of Italy – which was finally achieved in 1871.

20th Century and Beyond

Rapid growth and industrialisation characterised the post-unification period. Milan became the economic and cultural capital of Italy and over 50 years the population trebled in size. It was in Milan that Mussolini created the Fasci di Combattimento in 1919, the nucleus of the National Fascist Party. Following the fall of the socialist regime, Mussolini put Lake Garda on the political map by setting up his puppet republic in Salò in 1943, under the protection of a German army. In April 1945, just before the Allies reached Milan, *Il Duce* was finally captured at Dongo on Lake Como as he tried to flee to Switzerland. The following day he was executed along with 15 Nazi officials and his mistress, Clara Petacci. Their bodies were strung by their feet from the girders of a petrol station in Milan's Piazzale Loreto.

Villa Feltrinelli on Lake Garda, where Mussolini ruled from 1943–5

Following widespread destruction in World War II, Milan and the Lombard cities saw major reconstruction and rapid economic recovery. Milan became an industrial powerhouse, forming, with Genoa and Turin, the 'industrial triangle' of Italy. The city has emerged as Italy's leading centre for commerce, finance and publishing, and since the 1980s, as the country's capital of fashion. But alongside the economic boom came political scandal, organised crime and terrorism. On 12 December 1960 a bomb exploded in the city's Piazza Fontana, killing 16 and heralding a long period of terrorist activity. In the early 1990s Milan was the focus of the great political scandal dubbed *Tangentopoli* ('Bribesville'). Extensive investigations, known as the *Mani Pulite* (Clean Hands), exposed political corruption on a massive scale and led to the conviction of hundreds of politicians and businessmen.

Boat skipper

But despite corruption and crime, the region continues to flourish and the locals enjoy the highest standard of living in Italy. In the lakes region you are blissfully unaware of political wrangles – or the fact that Lombardy, where most of the lakes lie, is Italy's most industrial and populous region. It is no wonder that the city dwellers retreat here in summer – or that celebrities, in search of peace, have been snapping up villas on the quiet shores of Como.

Historical Landmarks

c.8000BC–3rd century BC Inhabitants of the Val Camonica, north of Lake Iseo, leave thousands of carvings on the rocks, illustrating prehistoric life.

202–191BC Romans start to establish colonies in Milan, Como, Brescia, Verona and other settlements.

222BC Romans conquer Milan (Mediolaum).

AD286 Milan becomes capital of the Western Roman Empire.

313 Constantine grants religious freedom to Christians in Milan.

568 Lombards invade Po Valley and lakes.

774 Charlemagne brings Lombard rule to an end.

11th century Emergence of the communes or city-states.

1118–27 Como defeated by Milan in the Ten Years War.

12th–15th century Milan ruled by the Viscontis and Sforzas; Lake Garda and Verona by the Scaligeri (della Scala) dynasty.

16th century Milan and the western lakes controlled by Spanish, the eastern lakes by the Venetian Empire.

1714 Spain cedes Lombardy to Austria.

1796 Napoleon invades. Milan becomes capital of the short-lived Cisalpine Republic.

1814–70 The Risorgimento – movement for the liberation and political unification of Italy.

1859 French defeat Austrians in the battles of Magenta and Solferino.

1870 Italy is unified under King Vittorio Emanuele II.

1921 Mussolini founds the National Fascist Party in Milan.

1943–5 Mussolini is installed as head of a puppet republic at Salò, Lake Garda. In 1945 he and his mistress, Claretta Petacci, are captured by partisans and executed.

2002 The euro replaces the lira as the official Italian currency.

2001–6 Media magnate Silvio Berlusconi heads the longest-serving Italian government since World War II.

2006 Romano Prodi's centre-left alliance wins a narrow victory over Berlusconi's right-wing Forza Italia.

WHERE TO GO

It is worth devoting a couple of weeks in order to experience the lakes region and the historic Lombard cities fully. The A4 autostrada provides a quick way of getting across the region by car, but the roads around the lakes can be very slow going. If you are without a car or your time is limited to a week or less, make your base at one of the larger lake resorts and take one or two relaxing ferry trips around the lakeshore. The Roman and Renaissance delights of Verona warrant an overnight stay.

LAKE MAGGIORE

Famed for its jewel-like islands and mountain-girt northern shores, Maggiore is the second largest of the Italian lakes. Long and narrow, it snakes 65km (40 miles) from the Swiss canton of Ticino in the north to Lombardy in the south. The western shore, where most of the main resorts are located, lies in Piedmont. The most scenic section of the lake is the Gulf of Borromeo, named after the family who have had a monopoly on Maggiore's star attractions for four and a half centuries.

> According to Stendhal, 'when a man has a heart and a shirt he should sell the shirt in order to see Lake Maggiore'. Byron, Shelley, Flaubert, Ruskin and Dickens were among other literati who sung the praises of the lake.

Stresa and the Golfo Borromeo

Stresa, 'Queen of the Lake', lies at the foot of the majestic Mottarone peak and boasts glorious views to the islands. Following the opening of the Simplon Pass in 1906, the town

The delightful fishing village of Malcesine on Lake Garda

became a highly fashionable resort, with splendid belle-époque villas and gardens, sports clubs and a casino. Today, huge old-fashioned hotels line its immaculate, garden-lined promenade. Foremost amongst these is the sumptuous Grand Hotel des Iles Borromées, whose star-studded guest list has included Queen Victoria, Churchill and Ernest Hemingway.

The resort may have lost the cachet it once enjoyed (today's visitors are more likely to be package tourists or conference delegates than royalty or celebrities) but as a base on the lake it still can't be beaten for views, excursions and easy access to the **Borromeo Islands**. It also has an appealing older quarter behind the waterfront where the narrow cobbled streets are lined by little shops and eateries, and the central, plane-shaded piazza buzzes with café life after dark.

From Stresa it's a quick ferry hop to **Isola Bella**, the first of the Borromeo Islands (open late Mar–late Oct daily 9am–5.30pm; admission fee, cumulative ticket available with Isola Madre; <www.borromeoturismo.it>). It was in the mid-16th century that Count Carlo III decided to transform the rocky islet (then known as Isola Inferiore) into a monumental baroque palace and gardens. He named it Isola Isabella after his wife, later shortened to Isola Bella (Beautiful Island). In the 17th century Carlo's son, Vitaliano, took over the project, commissioning leading architects and artists. It was not until 1959 however, that the scheme was finally complete.

To see the Borromeo Islands at a leisurely pace, you should allow a whole day – though a longish morning or afternoon may suffice. Bear in mind that in season the islands are inundated with crowds – the earlier you set off the better – and beware of boat touts near the main ferry landing stage charging far higher prices than the ferries.

Designed to give the impression of the prow of a

grandiose vessel, the island creates a dramatic impact as you approach by boat. The palace, terraces and gardens occupy almost the entire island, leaving just a cluster of houses near the harbour and a few souvenir shops. The stern facade belies a lavish interior, full of gilt and stuccowork, marble statues and Murano chandeliers. A tour takes in the Sala di Napoleone (Napoleon's Room) where he and Josephine slept in 1797. At lake level there are six mosaic grottoes, built by the Borromeans to avoid the stifling summer heat.

White peacock on Isola Bella

The garden is a baroque extravaganza of statuary, exotic plants and flowers. The ten ornate terraces culminate in a huge statue of a unicorn – one of the Borromeo symbols. Even if you find the grounds unbearably pompous you can't fail to admire the remarkable variety of exotic flora, planned to create colour and scent from early spring to late autumn – not to mention the sublime views across to the Mottarone peak.

A five minute ferry ride from Isola Bella brings you to **Isola dei Pescatori**, or – as you hear the ferry men announce it – 'Isola Superiore dei Pescatori'. The full name derives from the Latin *superior*, indicating that it is further north than Isola Bella ('Isola Inferiore'). The quaint, picturesque and laid-back Fishermen's Island couldn't be more of a contrast to formal Isola Bella. Heralded by the spire of its church, it is no more than a cluster of simple fishermen's houses and narrow alleys. At the end of the 19th century the population was around 200 and visitors were a rarity. Today there are 50 permanent residents. Despite the summer influx of tourists the island manages to preserve fishing traditions and is a lovely spot to stop for lunch and try the fish fresh from the lake *(see page 135)*.

The ferry stops at Baveno *(see page 30)* before arriving at the second of the Borromeo islands: **Isola Madre**. Different again, this one is a thickly wooded island, where English-style gardens dominate. The island has belonged to the Borromeo family since the 1500s and the glorious gardens were designed in the 19th century on what was formerly hunting ground. Peacocks and pheasants roam freely among the rare plants and exotic flora. Renowned for azaleas, rhododendrons and camellias, the gardens also nurture banana plants and sugar cane, lemon trees, magnolia, a Ginkgo biloba and

---

Lago Maggiore Express

The train-and-boat Lago Maggiore Express journey combines magnificent lake and mountain scenery. From Stresa you take a ferry to Locarno in Swiss Lake Maggiore (3hrs), then from here the Centovalli narrow-gauge railway takes you through scenic valleys to Domodossola (1½ hrs), returning to Stresa via the normal train service. The trip is taken independently and you can start at any point on the route. A one-day ticket easily suffices to cover the whole route, but two day tours are available if you want to spread out the journey, and these include a free lake pass for the extra day. The service runs from April to September, in April and May on Friday, Saturday, Sunday and holidays only, from June to late September daily except Wednesday. For information tel: 800-551801 within Italy, or consult <www.navigazione laghi.it>. Passports are required.

Wooded Isola Madre at dusk

a 200-year old Kashmir cypress tree, reputedly the largest in Europe. The palace is far less grandiose than its sister on Isola Bella. The rooms have been reconstructed and the interior has a mixed collection of Borromeo portraits, baroque allegorical paintings, tapestries, porcelain and puppets.

Monte Mottarone and Verbania

Between lakes Maggiore and Orta, the **Mottarone peak** is a natural balcony commanding a wonderful panorama of the lakes and the Alps; on one of those rare clear days you are said to be able to see seven lakes. Access is either by car (the last section is a toll road owned by the Borromeo family), foot (four hours along marked trails) or via the Mottarone cable car on the north side of Stresa (open daily 9.30am–5.30pm; admission fee; <www.stresa-mottarone.it>). Half way up, the cable car stops at the **Giardino Botanico Alpinia** (open Apr–Oct daily 9.30am–6pm; admission fee,

In the hills above Stresa, the village of Gignese is best known for the Museo dell'Ombrello e del Parasole (open Apr–Sep Tues–Sun 10am–noon, 3–6pm; admission fee; <www.gignese.it/museo/ombrello>). The museum displays 19th- and 20th-century umbrellas and parasols, and documents the life of the local umbrella-makers, some of whose descendants still make and repair umbrellas. Gignese is 8km (5 miles) from Stresa, on a road linking lakes Maggiore and Orta.

cumulative ticket with cable car available; <www.giardino alpinia.it>), an Alpine garden with over 1,000 species and fine lake views. The Mottarone is also popular with hang gliders and mountain bikers (bikes and helmets can be rented).

On the southern edge of Stresa the **Villa Pallavicino** (open Mar–Oct daily 9am–6pm; admission fee; <www.parcozoopallavicino.it>) has a 20-hectare (50-acre) park with botanical gardens and a collection of animals, some of which roam freely through the grounds. Only the gardens are open to the public.

Baveno is a smaller version of Stresa which became prosperous from the pink granite quarried from its slopes. This was used in Milan's Galleria Vittorio Emanuele II and St Paul's in Rome. Like Stresa, Baveno became fashionable in the 19th century, and in 1879 was visited by Queen Victoria. Rising above the village is the spire of the Church of Santi Gervasio e Protasio, which retains its Romanesque facade and an enchanting baptistery with frescoed vault and cupola.

Facing Stresa across the Gulf of Borromeo, suburban **Verbania** was created by Mussolini in 1939 to unite several communities, including Intra and Pallanza. By far the prettiest of these is **Pallanza**, where magnolias and oleanders line the quaysides and colourful cafés flank the piazzas. The resort has some fine villas and gardens, such as the famous **Villa Taranto**

(open end Mar–Oct daily 8.30am–5pm; <www.villataranto. it>) on the outskirts of town. In 1931 Neil McEacharn, a retired Scottish captain and passionate horticulturist, purchased the property and converted what was an unruly wooded headland into one of Europe's leading botanical gardens.

Twenty hectares (50 acres) are planted with around 20,000 different species of trees, shrubs and flowers, collected by McEacharn from five different continents, and notably Asia. A hundred gardeners were employed and the lake waters were used for irrigation. In 1952 the gardens were opened to the public and a new ferry stop, Villa Taranto, was created. McEacharn donated the complex to the state in 1938; he died here in 1964 and is buried in a mausoleum in the gardens. Eighty thousand tulips, 300 varieties of rhododendrons and a similar number of dahlias ensure colour from spring to autumn. Magnificent species of trees include cypress, sequoia,

The elaborate mausoleum at Villa Taranto

horse chestnuts from India and a splendid *Davidia Involucrata* (called the 'handkerchief tree' because of the white hanging squares it produces in spring). In the Victoria Amazonica Greenhouse the giant water lilies measure up to 2m (6½ft) and resemble huge green trays. The flowers, which are nocturnal, only live for around 48 hours and gradually change colour from creamy white to pink and purplish red.

Southern Lake Maggiore

South of Laveno on the east side of the lake, the enchanting little church of **Santa Caterina del Sasso** clings to a steep cliff face above the lake (open Apr–Oct 8.30am–noon, 2.30–6pm, March 9am–noon, 2–5pm, Nov–Feb weekends only; <www.provincia.va.it/santa caterina>). You can reach the church by taking a ferry or local boat, then climbing up the 80 steps from the landing stage; alternatively there is a steep 268-step climb down if you arrive by road.

Santa Caterina del Sasso

It was thanks to a local merchant and usurer (or so it is said) that the church was founded in the 12th century. Alberto Besozzi was saved from a shipwreck in 1170 and in thanksgiving spent the rest of his life praying in a cave by the rocks where he was washed ashore. His prayers were said to have saved the area from the plague and the locals built a votive chapel to Santa Caterina. This was enlarged to a monastery in the 14th century. Beautiful 14th–19th-century fresco cycles decorate the church and the Gothic chapterhouse.

In the 11th century the twin fortresses of **Arona** and **Angera** were built to safeguard the strategic southern part of the lake. Arona's is in ruins, but the **Rocca Borromeo** (open daily mid-Mar–mid-Oct 9am–5.30pm; admission fee; <www.borromeo turismo.it>) still dominates

The devil's in the detail at Rocca Borromeo

Angera. The castle became the property of the Visconti dynasty in the late 13th century, and was then purchased by the Borromeo family. The oldest wing features the Sala della Giustizia (Hall of Justice), decorated with 14th-century frescoes depicting the 1277 Visconti victory over the della Torres, which brought their dynasty to power. The fortress is also home to the Museo della Bambola, an outstanding doll museum.

The Rocca Borromeo looks across the lake to the ruined castle of **Arona**, on a rocky outcrop above the town. This was the birthplace of Saint Carlo Borromeo (1538–84), who was archbishop and cardinal of Milan and a key figure of the Counter-Reformation *(see box on page 18)*. Towering above the town is his huge copper statue, familiarly known as **San Carlone** (the big St Charles; open Apr–Sep 9am–12.30pm, 2–6.30pm, shorter hours off season). You can climb right up inside the statue, and look through his eyes, though this is not to be recommended on a hot summer's day. Arona itself is a large crowded town, with a few pleasant older parts and lake-view cafés, but generally unworthy of a detour.

The Northern Lake

The main resorts of the northern lake all lie on the sunny western shores. **Cannero Riviera** occupies a charming site amid subtropical flora, looking over to the picturesque ruins of the Malpaga castles. Lovely little **Cannobio**, last town before the Swiss border, has a long promenade and a delightful old quarter preserving its medieval character. In the nearby Val Cannobina, Orrido di Sant'Anna is a deep and dramatic gorge, carved out by the River Cannobino – a lovely spot for a picnic, or lunch perhaps at the restaurant Sant'Anna *(see page 136)*.

Locarno, the main resort of Swiss Lake Maggiore, is a sunny, southwest-facing town with a mild climate and flourishing parks and lakeside gardens. The heart of the town is the

A cobbled street in Cannobio

porticoed **Piazza Grande**, flanked by lively cafés and pizzerias where you can sit and watch the fashionable crowds go by. In summer this is the venue for open-air concerts, and in August an outdoor screen is set up for the International Film Festival. Southwest of the piazza, the 14th-century but much-restored Castello Visconteo is

A fifth of Lake Maggiore lies in the Swiss Canton of Ticino. If you are visiting the northern Swiss lake from Italy don't forget your passport and some Swiss currency. Euros are widely accepted, but you will receive change in Swiss francs, often at a poor exchange rate.

home to the Museo Archeologico, noted for its Roman remains. Up from Piazza Grande, the old town has some handsome villas, churches and the Casa Rusca art museum, with work by the French artist Jean Arp and his contemporaries.

For wonderful views of the lake and Alps take the funicular or walk up to the **Santuario della Madonna del Sasso** (open daily 6.30am–7pm) above the resort. You can go on up from here via a glass and steel cable car to the panoramic plateau of Cardada (1,350m/4,429ft; <www.cardada.ch>). A 10-minute walk and a chairlift will take you higher still to Cimetta (1,670m/5,480ft), with even more staggering views.

Across the Maggia River from Locarno lies the smaller town of **Ascona**. This is another fashionable resort, and traditionally a magnet for writers and artists. Paul Klee, Hermann Hesse, Isadora Duncan and Jung were among those who were lured by its charms. Klee was one of several artists in the 1920s who donated works to the **Museo di Comunale d'Arte Moderna** (Museum of Modern Art, Via Borgo 34; open Tues–Sat 10am–noon, 3–6pm, Sun 4–6pm; admission fee). Ascona's natural magnet is the lakefront promenade, with views across the water to the Isole di Brissago, the tiny twin islands which you can visit by boat either from Ascona or Locarno.

LAKE COMO

Celebrated since ancient times for its great natural location, Como is the most dramatic and romantic of the three great lakes. Shaped like an inverted Y, it has three branches which meet at the Punta Spartivento ('the Point that divides the Wind'), the seductive setting of the enchanting resort of Bellagio. Of the lower two branches the Ramo di Como or western branch is the most scenic, its shores studded with villas, gardens and picturesque harbours and villages. The eastern branch, known as the Lago di Lecco, is more stark and rugged and has at its southern tip the large industrial centre of Lecco.

Although the lake is smaller than Maggiore and Garda, it has the longest perimeter at 170km (106 miles). It is also the deepest lake in Italy and one of the deepest in Europe (410m or 1,358ft at its deepest point). In the centre, useful car-ferry services link the resorts of Menaggio, Bellagio and Caden-

Sons of Como

Como's most famous sons were Pliny the Elder (AD23–79), the Roman scholar who wrote the 37-volume *Historia Naturalis* (Natural History) and died during the eruption of Vesuvius in AD79, and his nephew and adopted son, Pliny the Younger (AD61–113), an author and lawyer who left a large collection of private letters offering a fascinating insight into public and private life of the times. The same Pliny is said to have owned at least two villas at Bellagio, one on the hilltop for study and reflection (possibly on the site of the current Villa Serbelloni), and another on the lakeshore for hunting and fishing.

Como's most famous scientist was Alessandro Volta (1745–1827), who invented the battery and after whom the volt is named. The neoclassical Volta Temple on Como's waterfront houses a collection of his instruments and inventions.

abbia, saving a lot of mile-
age and some hair-raising
driving. (The road from Bellagio to Como is very narrow and precipitous).

Como Town

A large industrial centre and
transport hub, Como may not
be the obvious choice for a
lakeside base. But it has a
fine lakeshore setting, an historic quarter with cobbled,
traffic-free streets, some lively cafés and shops selling the
famous Como silk, as well as

Basilica di San Fedele

jewellery and leather. The Piazza del Duomo in the centre is a
natural magnet. The square is dominated by the lavishly sculpt-
ed facade of the **Duomo** (open daily 7am–noon, 3–7pm). A
fusion of Gothic and Renaissance, with a dome added in 1744,
the church took some 350 years to complete. The portal is
flanked by niche statues of Pliny the Elder (on the left) and
Pliny the Younger (on the right) – surprising since both Plinys
were pagans. The interior is full of works of art, including Renaissance tapestries hanging in the nave and paintings by Gau-
denzio Ferrari (c.1471/81–1546) and Bernardino Luini (1480–
1532), two Lombard painters influenced by Leonardo.

Next to the Duomo is the lovely arcaded **Broletto**, the former Court of Justice, built in 1251, at the same time as the
adjacent Torre del Comune (clock tower). The **Basilica di
San Fedele** (open daily 8am–noon, 3.30–7pm) stands on the
nearby Piazza Fedele, an attractive medieval square with
porticoed houses. The Lombard-Romanesque church has
been much altered over the centuries and was given a new

facade in the early 20th century. Originally Como's cathedral, the church was the work of the *Maestri Comacini*, medieval stonemasons of Como renowned throughout Europe for their craftsmanship. Another example of their work is the Romanesque gem of **Sant'Abbondio** (Via Sant'-Abbondio, out of the centre; open daily 7am–6pm), with a remarkable cycle of mid-14th century frescoes in the apse, depicting scenes from the *Life of Christ*.

The Comaschi (citizens of Como) have been producing silk and other textiles since the 15th century and the town is the centre of Italy's silk industry. Silkworms are no longer bred here, but Chinese fibres are imported to be woven, dyed and printed. Armani, Hermes and Versace are just three of the famous designers who depend on Como for their silk. The small **Museo Didattico della Seta** (Silk Museum, Via Castelnuovo 1; open Tues–Fri 9am–noon, 3–6pm; admis-

All aboard at Como waterfront

sion fee; <www.museoseta
como.com>) on the edge of
town documents the story of
Como's silk, with sections
on silkworm breeding and
silk-making processes.

For a bird's-eye view of
the town take the **Brunate
cable car** which rises up the
hillside east of the centre. In
seven minutes you are at the
hilltop village of Brunate

> A ferry trip is the best
> way to see the lake.
> Coastal roads that
> plunge you into dimly
> lit tunnels and are often
> traffic-clogged in season
> do not make for relax-
> ing driving; what's
> more, many of the
> lake's loveliest features
> are only visible from
> the water.

where you can enjoy views across the lake to the Alps.
Brunate can also be reached on foot from Como, and makes
a good starting point for hikes in the hills.

Ramo di Como

The Como branch of the lake, known as the **Ramo di Como**,
is best seen by boat. You can travel either by *Battello*, the regular ferry boat which stops at all the landing stages; by *Alis-
cafo*, the faster hydrofoil which makes fewer stops; or by
excursion cruiser. Boats depart from Piazza Cavour in central
Como and tickets can be purchased from kiosks on the lakefront. From Como to Bellagio the boats afford splendid views
of the villages tumbling down the steep wooded hillsides and
the neoclassical villas and gardens overlooking the lake.

The first main stop is **Cernobbio**, famous for the grandiose villas built here in the 16th to 18th centuries. Best
known among them is the **Villa d'Este**, which since 1873
has been the most luxurious hotel on the lake *(see page 130)*.
It was built in the 16th century for Cardinal Tolomeo Gallio,
Secretary of State to Pope Gregory XIII and at one time was
home of Caroline of Brunswick (1768–1821), the disgraced
and estranged wife of George Frederick, who later became

King George IV of England. Since becoming a hotel the villa has hosted royalty, politicians and film stars. Some of Cernobbio's splendid villas have been converted to conference or exhibition centres, such as the 19th-century Villa Erba; others are owned by wealthy businessmen or celebrities – the most recent arrival is George Clooney, who has bought a lakeside villa at the village of Laglio further along the coast. At the romantic little village of Moltrasio, 3km (2 miles) north of Cernobbio, **Le Fontanelle** was the weekend retreat of the late designer, Gianni Versace. This was the favourite of his four homes – and the one where he chose to be buried. The villa was regularly visited by a string of celebrities, Madonna and Elton John among them.

> **Villa del Balbianello** (gardens open Easter–Oct, Tues and Thur–Sun 10am–12.30pm, 3.30–6.30pm; for the villa tel: 0344 56110; admission fee; <www.fondoambiente.it>) also attained celebrity status recently when its grounds were used as a location in the James Bond movie *Casino Royale*. It stands in an enchanting setting on the wooded headland south of Lenno. To see inside the villa you have to take an organised tour from Como, but the gardens alone are worth a visit. A private shuttle boat service runs from Lenno jetty. Alternatively, on a Tuesday, Saturday or Sunday you can go by foot from Lenno (about 1km), signed from the church square.

Built as a retreat in 1787 by Cardinal Angelo Maria Durini, the villa incorporates the remains of a Franciscan convent, which you can still see at the lower level. The eccentric cardinal led a life of study and contemplation, sleeping between black sheets in a black bedroom with a coffin beside his bed to remind him of his fate. One of Durini's descendants, Count Guido Monzino, acquired the property in 1954. On his death he left the villa and contents to the FAI, the Fondo Ambiente Italiano, Italy's equivalent of the National Trust. Monzino, who led a North Pole expedition in 1971 and the first successful

Italian ascent of Everest in 1973, used the villa as an international centre for the study of explorations. As well as some fine English antiques, ceramics, paintings and *objets d'art*, there is a library with hundreds of books devoted to mountaineering and polar expeditions, a map-reading room used to plan the expeditions and a museum full of Monzino's mountaineering memorabilia. The gardens, climbing up the headland, combine magnificent oaks, cypresses and plane trees with immaculate lawns, romantic paths and pergolas. The climax is the open loggia at the top with glorious vistas of the lake.

In the lee of the promontory the **Isola Comacina** is the only island of the lake. Tiny though it is, the settlement was fortified by the Romans and became a political and military centre in the Middle Ages, acquiring the name of Crispoli, City of Gold. The islanders supported Milan in its destruction of Como in 1128 and in retaliation Como ravaged the island in 1169, forc-

The late 18th-century Villa del Balbianello featured in *Casino Royale*

ing them to take refuge in Varenna. The baroque Oratorio di San Giovanni and the ruins of medieval churches are all that remain. The island was bequeathed to the King of Belgium in 1914, later donated to the state and today is under the supervision of the Brera Academy of Fine Arts in Milan. A handful of artists live in cottages here. The Locanda dell'Isola Comacina dishes out an expensive lunch to tourists *(see page 138)*. Alternatively, there are plenty of peaceful spots for a picnic.

Centro Lago (The Central Lake)

Grand old villas and luxuriant gardens line the lakeshores at Tremezzo. The most famous among them is **Villa Carlotta** (open daily Apr–Sep 9am–6pm, Oct–Mar and Nov 9am–11.30pm, 2–4.30pm; <www.villacarlotta.it>; admission fee), a vast neo-classical pile graced by over 5.6 hectares (14 acres) of gardens, and famous for its numerous varieties and huge species of azaleas and rhododendrons. The villa was built from 1690–1743 by the Clerici, a wealthy Milanese family of merchants. Most of the contents you see today were acquired by the following owner, Giambattista Sommariva. His political arch rival, Duke Francesco Melzi d'Eril, meanwhile constructed a beautiful villa in Bellagio,

Villa Carlotta

right opposite Villa Carlotta. Competition between them led to continual embellishment of both residences and gardens. In 1843 Villa Carlotta was acquired by Princess Marianna of the Netherlands, wife of Prince Albert of Prussia, who gave the villa to her daughter, Carlotta, as a wedding present – hence its present name.

The villa has a magnificent entrance with a grand stairway, gardens, balustrades and fountains. The interior, a bit of an anti climax after the gardens, is decorated with Empire furniture and neoclassical and romantic sculpture and painting. There are works by Canova, though the much-vaunted *Cupid and Psyche* is a copy of the original which is in the Louvre.

Bellagio, 'pearl of the lake', enjoys an unrivalled setting on the wooded promontory that divides the Lecco and Como arms of the lake. Walks around the cape afford sublime views of mountains in all directions, and notably north to the often snowcapped mountains along the Swiss border. The impossibly picturesque old town (or *borgo*) retains its medieval layout with porticos, cobbled alleys and stepped streets leading up from the waterside. Enticing cafés, where you can sip a cocktail and watch the ferries plying across the lake, stretch out along the waterfront. All of this of course draws boatloads of tourists throughout the season, but it is enchanting nonetheless. Ideally stay a night or two and enjoy the village after dusk when the day-trippers have departed.

The commercial city of Lecco, on the southern tip of Lago di Lecco, is famous as the centrepiece of Alessandro Manzoni's masterpiece *I Promessi Sposi* (The Betrothed), published in 1827. Manzoni memorabilia can be seen at his childhood home, and locations from his novel can be identified in the town and surrounding landscape.

On the hill behind the village are the gardens of the **Villa Serbelloni** (guided tours only, starting from the medieval tower in Piazza della Chiesa; Apr–Oct Tues–Sun at 11am and 4pm; admission fee). The villa, not to be confused with the exclusive hotel of the same name on the lakeside, belongs to the Rockefeller Foundation and is not open to the public. The steep path takes you well above the villa for sublime lake and mountain panoramas. On the south side of the village are the exotic gardens of **Villa Melzi** (open Mar–early Nov 9am–6pm; admission fee), which spill down to the lake. The fine, if faded, neoclassical palace (closed to the public) was built for Francesco Melzi d'Eril, vice-president of Napoleon's Cisalpine Republic.

Setting off from Bellagio, passenger boats, hydrofoils and car ferries ply across the lake to Menaggio and Varenna. On the western side of the lake, **Menaggio** is larger than Bellagio and not quite as picturesque, but it has its charms and makes an excellent base for boat trips and trekking in the hills. Large, belle-époque hotels are peacefully set along the lakeside promenade, restaurant terraces make the most of the views and there's a lively little centre with bars, small shops and a well-stocked tourist office. Golf, rockclimbing, riding, tennis, cycling, water-skiing, windsurfing

Varenna's waterfront

and canoeing are just a few of the activities on offer – and there's a good beach and large pool at the Lido. Serious trekkers might consider the Alta Via del Lario, the route that winds from Menaggio to Gera Lario, following high ground along the Swiss border.

Varenna, across the lake, is a perfectly preserved medieval village where narrow stepped alleys lead down to a romantic lakeside walkway, shaded by porticos and arbours. In many ways this little gem is just as charming as Bellagio, but far less crowded and commercialised. Moreover, it has a number of excellent little hotels and restaurants, and two lakeside villas with gardens open to the public.

With the Allied troops approaching in 1945, Mussolini, who had been head of the puppet republic of Salò, was forced to flee. He was on his way to board a plane for Switzerland with his mistress, Clara Petacci, when he was captured by Italian communist partisans at Dongo, on the northern reaches of Lake Como. The following day they were executed and their bodies taken to Milan to be strung up in Piazzale Loreto.

Villa Monastero (open Apr–Oct daily 9am–6pm, except when conferences are in progress; admission fee; <www.villamonastero.org>) is a former Cistercian convent founded in 1208 by nuns who escaped from Isola Comacina when the island was sacked by Como. The villa, transformed into an aristocratic residence in the 17th century, is now an international cultural and scientific centre, but you can visit the beautiful terraced gardens spilling down to the lake. The neighbouring **Villa Cipressi** gardens (open Apr–Oct 9am–6pm) are also open to the public, and the villa is now a hotel.

Ramo di Colico

The northern branch of the lake, called the **Ramo di Colico** or Alto Lario, has no resorts of great charm but you may like to visit the **Abbazia di Piona** (open daily in season 8.30am–12.30pm, 1.30–7pm; admission fee). This 11th-century abbey has a pretty setting on the tip of the Olgiasca promontory enclosing the small bay of Lake Piona. The abbey was founded by Cluniac monks but is now home to Cistercians. The ruins of the Lombard Romanesque church retain early frescoes and there are beautiful Gothic/Renaissance cloisters (1252). The monks are famous for their home-made strong brews which are sold in the shop here. The abbey can be accessed by ferry in summer.

LAKE GARDA

The largest and easternmost of the lakes, Garda is bordered by three different regions: Lombardy, Trentino and the Veneto. The scenery is enormously diverse, from the fjord-like north, where the Brenta Dolomites drop sheer into the water, to the gentle hills of vineyards and olive groves, and the sealike southern basin, fringed by beaches. Sheltered by the mountains, it enjoys an equable climate and luxuriant vegetation along its shores. Garda is the cleanest lake and the most popular for swimming, windsurfing and sailing. The lake is a favourite playground of German and Austrian tourists and in season you can expect crowded campsites and coachloads of day-trippers, particularly in the south.

Rocca Scaligeri

The Southern Shores

Sirmione, Lake Garda's most famous resort, has an enticing setting on a narrow peninsula that juts 4km (2½ miles) into the lake. The old town is heralded by the photogenic **Rocca Scaligera** (Scaligera Castle; open Tues–Sun 8.30am–7pm, off season 9am–4.30pm; admission fee), accessed via a drawbridge over the fish-filled moat. The castle was built in 1259 by Mastino I della Scala, the fishtail battlements being the trademark of the della Scala family. The narrow alleys around the castle teem with tourists throughout the season – Sirmione is just minutes away from the Milan–Venice motorway and a mecca for day-trippers. But beyond the castle you can escape the worst of the crowds and find pleasant lakeside terraces, beaches and a headland of olive trees and cypresses. At the tip of the peninsula lies the famous **Grotte de Catullo** (open Mar–mid Oct Tues–Sun 8.30am–7pm, mid-Oct–Feb Tues–Sun 8.30am–4.30pm; admission fee), the ruins of a vast Roman villa. The site was named after the Roman poet Catullus, but although his poems make reference to a home in Sirmione there is no evidence this was his villa. The archaeological remains – some of the most important of their kind in Italy – cover over 2 hectares (5 acres) of the promontory, and are set high above the lake amid olive and cypress trees. Deciphering the various rooms on the various levels is not easy, but it is lovely just to wander around.

Venetian-style house in Desenzano del Garda

West of Sirmione, **Desenzano del Garda** is the largest town on the lake, and one of the most colourful and lively. An important Roman port, it retains a 3rd-century **Villa Romana** (open Mar–mid-Oct Tues–Sat 8.30am–7pm, Sun 9am 5pm, mid Oct–Feb Tues–Sat 8.30am–4.30pm, Sun 9am–4.30pm; admission fee) with remarkable floor mosaics depicting scenes of hunting and local life. The heart of the town is the picturesque **Porto Vecchio** (Old Port) flanked by cafés and the venue of a large and popular Tuesday market. Behind the port, narrow lanes lead up to the medieval castle (currently under restoration), while along the front, the promenade is pleasant for strolling.

Sirmione has been a spa since Roman times. Large numbers of visitors come to its thermal establishment for treatment from the sulphurous water that comes from a spring in the lake (<www.termedi sirmione.com>).

East of Sirmione, **Peschiera del Garda** was a medieval stronghold of the Venetian empire. The town is still dominated by the mighty bastions of its fortress, but there is not a great deal to detain you here. Nowadays, Peschiera is associated more with amusement parks than history. **Gardaland** *(see page 93)* is Italy's number one theme park, boasting 46-hectares (113 acres) of Disneyland-styled attractions, and **Canevaworld** *(see page 94)* comprises the large Aqua Paradise waterpark and Movieland Studios.

The Western Shore

North of Desenzano the town of **Salò** has a long history dating back to Roman times. In 1337 it became the capital of the Magnifica Patria, a community of 42 towns; during a less-fortunate episode in the town's history, it became the seat of Mussolini's puppet republic in 1943 – his last desperate attempt to reorganise Fascism in Italy. The Art Nouveau-style Villa Simonini (now the Hotel Laurin) was the head-quarters of the Italian Foreign Ministry, presided over by *Il Duce*. On a beautiful deep bay, and backed by the Monte San Bartolomeo, Salò is an appealing combination of bustling local town and elegant resort – with no hint of its dubious history. The narrow streets and squares of the historic quarter lie behind a long lakeside promenade. The late-Gothic **Duomo** (open daily 8.30am–noon, 3–6.30pm) along the waterfront, spied from afar by its distinctive bell tower, has an unfinished brick facade, with a Renaissance portal. The piazza here is the setting for summer performances of the Gasparo da Salò Festival of Music, celebrating the inventor (or perfecter) of the violin, born here in 1540.

Off the headland south of Salò lies the little, cypress-studded island of **Isola del Garda**. In private hands for several centuries, the island was inherited by Camillo Cavazza and the current residents are his English wife (who personally gives the guided tours) and her seven children. Boats leave from Salò and Gardone Riviera three times a week (Mon, Wed and Fri) and tours include the neo-Gothic villa and fine gardens, with tastings of local products such as wine and olive oil.

Tignale and Tremósine

Well worth a diversion from the coast is the panoramic route climbing up to Tignale and Tremósine, scenic plateaux of alpine meadows. (Note, though, that the narrow roads and hairpin bends are not for the faint-hearted). The 43-km (27-mile) detour from the lake starts on the road 4km (2½ miles) north of Gargnano. This snakes its way up to Tignale (555m/1,821ft), then descends before climbing up again to the Tremósine plateau – an even higher balcony commanding views of the entire lake basin. From here the main road comes down to join the lake at Limone del Garda.

Just along the coast, **Gardone Riviera** maintains much of the elegance that drew royalty and wealthy international visitors in the late 19th and early 20th centuries. The Austrian Emperor and other European elite built palatial villas here and Gardone became the most fashionable resort on the lake. Among the eminent guests at the belle-époque Grand Hotel, which still stands on the waterfront, were Somerset Maugham, Nabokov and

View from Tignale

Churchill. Further along, at the Villa Fiordaliso, Mussolini stayed with his mistress Clara Petacci during the Salò Republic. This lovely Art Nouveau lakeside villa is now a hotel and restaurant where you can enjoy fine cuisine on the lake.

But the biggest draw of Gardone, particularly for Italian day-trippers, is **Il Vittoriale degli Italiani**, (park and gardens open daily 8.30am–8pm; guided tours of house and War Museum; admission fee; <www.vittoriale.it>). This eccentric residence, set in 9 hectares (22 acres) of gardens with lake views, was home to the flamboyant poet, dramatist, soldier and socialite, Gabriele d'Annunzio (1863–1938). The memorabilia from wartime, literary, artistic and womanising pursuits – not to mention the vast wedding cake mausoleum – are all a celebration of the man himself. Among the eccentricities are the coffin in the spare bedroom, the dark or painted windows (D'Annunzio hated daylight), an embalmed tortoise which died of overeating and the prow of the battleship, *Puglia*, wedged into the hillside.

Palms and bamboo, Giardino Botanico Hruska

In the early 20th century Arturo Hruska, a botanist and dentist to the last Tsar of Russia, transformed the sloping site above the town into an oasis of flora. The **Giardino Botanico Hruska** (open March–Oct daily 9am–7pm; admission fee) contains flourishing Alpine, subtropical and Mediterranean species. It's a wonderfully peaceful spot where you can wander among pretty rockeries, lush lawns, Japanese-style gardens, streams and waterfalls.

Toscalano-Maderno north of Gardone is the main embarkation point for the car ferry to Torri del Benaco. Going north, **Gargnano** is one of the main sailing centres on the lake and it is hard to find a more pleasant lakeside place to stay. Remarkably unspoilt, it has a lively little port, a promenade of orange trees, a couple of very enticing hotels *(see page 132)* and a gourmet restaurant serving some of the best cuisine on the lake *(see page 139)*.

The picturesque little town of **Limone Sul Garda** is by-passed by the main coast road, but heaves with tourists all through the season. The rows of white stone pillars of the now-defunct lemon terraces or *limonaie* are testimony to the citrus-fruit industry which made Limone rich. The trade declined in the 20th century with competition from cheaper citrus fruits grown in the hotter climate of the south. Fruit trees still flourish and market stalls brim with bottles of lemon liqueur, lemon-shaped ceramics and the freshly picked fruits. You might assume the village is named after the citrus fruit but it is more likely that it derives from the Latin *limen* or border, referring to the former frontier here between Austria and Italy.

Garda Trentino

The northern tip of the lake lies in Trentino, which was under Austrian rule from 1815–1918. Set against the dramatic backdrop of Monte Brione, the main resort of **Riva del Garda** has been luring visitors from the north since the 19th century. Today it is a thriving holiday resort, attracting a large number of German and British tourists, but managing to retain much of its former character and elegance. Strategically located between Verona and the Alps, the town was a major trading port, coveted by rival factions and variously acquired by the Veronese Scaligeri (1349), the Viscontis of Milan (1380) and the Venetian Republic (1440). The moated

---

Limone's Elixir of Life

In the late 1980s scientists discovered that many of Limone's inhabitants had a mystery protein in their blood that declogs their arteries of fat and gives them virtual immunity to heart attacks and strokes. The chemical, called Apolipoprotein A-1 Milano (shortened to Apo A-1 Milano) has been identified in around three dozen Limonesi. The mutant gene has been passed from generation to generation – Limone was an isolated village pre-1932, only accessible by boat or by crossing the mountains, and intermarriage was common. All the carriers are descendants from the same couple who married in the 17th century. Apo A-1 Milano has attracted interest from scientists all over the world; and in case you're wondering, no link has (yet) been established between the protein and Limone lemons.

Monte Baldo cable car

La Rocca, dominating the waterfront and accessed over a drawbridge, is testimony to the Scaligera era. Since it was built in 1124 the castle has been remodelled several times, and under the Austrians the tower was truncated and the castle became a garrison. Today it is home to the Museo Civico, with displays of art and archaeology and occasional temporary exhibitions. Overlooking the harbour, **Piazza III Novembre** is the appealing main square, flanked by medieval Renaissance *palazzi* and the lofty Torre Apponale (great views from the top if it happens to be open). The tower has variously served as a prison, a store for salt and grain, and as a look-out point during World War I.

Cafés and pizzerias along the waterfront make the most of the views, and there are parks, gardens and pebbly beaches. The waters are dotted with windsurfers and dinghies all year round – you can rent equipment and have lessons, or just take a leisurely stroll along the waterfront to admire the views. You can walk all the way to **Torbole** (4km/2½ miles), described by Goethe as 'a wonder of nature, an enchanting sight'. Its setting below sheer rocks and beside the River Sarca is as alluring as ever, but the village is spoilt by the main road cutting off the centre from the lake, and unless you're into mountain climbing and windsurfing or sailing there is little to detain you.

The Eastern Shore

Stretching 50km (31 miles) along the eastern bank of the lake, the so-called Riviera degli Olivi is typified by tourist development as well as olive groves and vine-clad hills. The main road, known as the Gardesana Orientale, hugs the shoreline and is frequently traffic-clogged in summer. The northern section, between Torbole and Malcesine, has a series of dimly lit tunnels, plunging you from dazzling bright sunlight into blackness.

The resort of **Malcesine** lies at the foot of Monte Baldo, and clusters beneath the striking Castello Scaligero. This fishing village-turned-tourist magnet is a picturesque maze of cobbled alleys, with medieval porticoes and a small port which buzzes with activity throughout the season. A natural history museum is contained within the **castle** (open daily 9.30am–7pm, 8pm in summer; admission fee) and there are good views from the battlements and tower. Behind the resort the panoramic rotating cabins of a cable car whisk you up **Monte Baldo** (2,218m/7,275ft) in 10 minutes (open daily 8am–6pm; admission fee; <www.funivia malcesine.com>). (The cabins can also accommodate mountain bikes and hang gliders so you can freewheel or float back.) The ridge offers some ravishing **views** and scenic walking trails. In winter the cable car takes you to the ski slopes. Malcesine is a mecca for all sports

> The Sala Goethe in Malcesine's castle is devoted to the German writer's drawings, notes and views on Lake Garda and the castle. While compiling his *Travels in Italy* he visited the lake in 1786 when it was under Austrian rule. The writer was sketching the castle at Malcesine when he was arrested as an Austrian spy. He was imprisoned here but soon released after convincing the authorities of his innocence.

enthusiasts: apart from hiking, mountain biking and winter sports, there is windsurfing, kitesurfing, sailing and scubadiving on the lake, and tennis and horse riding on the shores.

Yet another Scaligeri castle heralds the town of **Torri del Benaco**. Views from the tower encompass almost the entire lake, from Sirmione to Limone. The castle museum is devoted to Torri's ancient way of life: boat building, fishing and olive cultivation. Modern Torri is busy with car ferries that ply across the waters to Toscolano-Maderno, but the old port has maintained its original character, and the Hotel Gardesana's Buonricordo Restaurant *(see page 140)*, which overlooks it, is a delightful spot for a relaxing drink or meal.

In ancient times Lake Garda was called 'Benacus' (beneficent) – and it is occasionally still referred to by the Latin name. The lake took its current name from the town of **Garda** which lies below a huge rocky outcrop on the southeastern shore. The town today is a bustling holiday resort where life focuses on a long, spacious promenade, lined by tourist cafés. Behind the waterfront the narrow alleys of the old quarter are packed with small shops, souvenirs and trattorias. **Punta San Vigilio** to the west is a delightful spot,

---

Monte Baldo

The 35-km (22-mile) mountain chain of Monte Baldo is famous for its profusion and variety of flora. Way back in the 16th century it became known for its rare botanical species and was visited by scholars of botany and herbalists working for European royal courts. Specialists have been exploring ever since, and now there are around 20 species which have *Baldense* as part of their official name. Among the species unique to the high ridge are *Anemone baldensis* (known as the Mount Baldo windrose) and *Veronica bonarota*.

where an ancient lane of cypresses leads to the tip of a peaceful promontory with a little church and a 16th-century villa. On a tiny harbour the Locanda San Vigilio, with just 7 rooms, has been welcoming guests since the early 16th century. On the other side of the promontory the Baia delle Sirene (Bay of the Sirens) has a good but crowded beach and is a pretty spot to take a picnic in the shade of olive trees.

South of Garda **Bardolino** offers plenty of opportunities for tasting the eponymous wine. Head for the **Museo del Vino** above the town (open mid-March–

Barrels of wine in Bardolino

end Oct daily 9am–1pm, 2–6pm; <www.zeni.it>) where you can try the local reds, whites and rosés, and purchase bottles at very reasonable prices. In late September and early October Bardolino hosts the Festa dell'Uva (Grape Festival) where corks pop nonstop. Wines aside, Bardolino is a pleasant lakeside resort with a tree-lined promenade and a centre boasting a profusion of small bars and cafés and two ancient churches. At Cisano di Bardolino the **Museo dell'Olio di Oliva** (Olive Oil Museum; open Mon–Sat 9am–12.30pm, 2.30–7pm, Sun 9am–12.30pm; <www.museo.com>) offers free tasting of local olive oil and has a little shop selling vinegars, olives, honey, pasta and pesto, as well as olive oil.

LESSER LAKES

Lake Orta

The westernmost of the lakes and the only one entirely in Piedmont territory, **Lake Orta** is just 14km (9 miles) long and 3km (2 miles) at its widest point. It may not sound that small but it's minute in comparison to neighbouring Maggiore, and a lot more peaceful. The highlight is **Orta San Giulio**, a perfectly preserved medieval village with mesmerising views over **Isola San Giulio**. This little island in the centre of the lake seems to float on the morning mist, and by night it's illuminated and every bit as magical.

Orta San Giulio positively oozes charm, with its cobbled, car-free alleys, ancient houses and enticing lakeside **Piazza Motta**. Nicknamed the *salotto* or drawing room, the square is overlooked by the lovely Palazzotto, the old town hall, with its loggia and faded frescoes. The little harbour is a scene of con-

The village of Orta San Giulio is closed to traffic and, unless you are unloading at a hotel, cars must be left in the paying car parks outside the centre. From here you can take an electric tourist train to the central piazza. Avoid visiting the lake on Sundays when coachloads of tourists descend on the village.

stant activity with rowing boats and water taxis plying back and forth to the island. Legend has it that San Giulio, a missionary from the Greek island of Aegina, rid the island of dragons and snakes in the 4th century and founded the basilica here. It was rebuilt in the 10th century and became a centre of pilgrimage. Though much remodelled since, the church

Fresco in the Basilica San Giulio

retains its richly carved, 11th-century black-marble pulpit, frescoes from four centuries and the remains of the saint. From the basilica a peaceful cobbled path, called the Way of Silence going in one direction and The Way of Meditation in the other, circuits the island, passing a Benedictine monastery (no public access) and private villas overlooking the lake.

On a hill above Orta San Giulio are the 21 chapels of the **Sacro Monte** (Holy Mount; <www.sacromonteorta.it>), decorated with 17th- and 18th-century frescoes and life-size terracotta figures illustrating scenes from the life of St Francis. Even if you don't make it to all the chapels, this is a lovely location with lake views and a welcoming little restaurant (the Sacro Monte).

Varese and its Lake

Prosperous **Varese** is essentially a modern city and manufacturing centre which, given all the attractions of nearby lakes Como and Maggiore, is largely ignored by tourists. In its favour are the Art Nouveau villas, parks and gardens (it is styled *Citta Giardino* or City of Gardens), sophisticated shopping and small historic centre. The Bernascone bell-

Known also by the Italians as Lake Ceresio, its ancient name, the many-fingered Lake Lugano lies deep in the mountains between lakes Como and Maggiore. Just over a third of the shore belongs to Italy, the rest to the Swiss canton of Ticino. The steep wooded hills rising sheer from the water preclude development along most of its shores and lively, stylish Lugano is the only large town, with sunny lakeside promenades, café-lined piazzas, luxury shops and galleries.

tower rises 77m (253ft) above the centre; beside it the Basilica of San Vittore (1580–1615) was later given a neoclassical facade; and behind it the Baptistery of San Giovanni, with some remarkable 14th century frescoes, is one of the few surviving buildings from the medieval town. North of the town don't miss **Villa Panza** (<www.fondoambiente.it>), a beautiful 18th-century villa and gardens, which houses a major collection of modern American art that belonged to the last owner of the villa, Giuseppe Panza.

The **Sacro Monte** is a major pilgrimage site 8km (5 miles) northwest of Varese on the wooded slopes of Monte Campo dei Fiori. Along the steep Via Sacra are 14 devotional chapels with life-size terracotta figures and frescoes. From the Sanctuary of Santa Maria del Monte and its village at the top there are fine views – and even better ones if you were to carry on 5km (3 miles) to the Parco Naturale di Campo dei Fiori.

Shaped like a battered boot, **Lago di Varese** is a tiny lake west of the city. This is a gentle, undramatic lake framed in rolling hills; the tiny wooded island off the west shore has a restaurant and the little Museum of Prehistory.

South of Varese, sitting among the industries of the Olona valley (and very poorly signed), is the Renaissance gem of **Castiglione Olona**. Cardinal Branda Castiglioni (1350–1443) created this beautiful complex by bringing the new Renaissance style from Tuscany to his native village. The leading Florentine artist, Masolino, was commissioned to decorate the buildings and there are stunning frescoes depicting the *Life of the Virgin* (1428) in the collegiate church above the old quarter and the *Life of John the Baptist* (1435) in the nearby baptistery.

Lake Iseo

Between the provinces of Bergamo and Brescia, **Lake Iseo** is comparatively tranquil and unknown. It lacks the picturesque villages of the larger lakes but has a fine setting within a ring of wooded mountains. Taking centre stage is **Monte Isola**, a large, car-free island with chestnut woods, vineyards, olive groves and a population of around 200, living in sleepy mountain and lakeside villages. A mecca for day-trippers, the island offers pleasant walks, bike rides and restaurants serving fish straight out of the surrounding waters. The lake's speciality is *tinca* (tench) served with polenta, or you could be offered crayfish, trout, pike or perch, washed down perhaps with one of the local Franciacorta sparkling white wines. **Iseo** is the lake's main town, and though very tourist-focused, retains a certain charm with its fine promenade and maze

View towards Monte Isola

A Franciacorta vineyard

of narrow lanes. **Sarnico** is a popular sports centre and has an attractive old quarter of narrow streets, small squares and arcaded houses. **Lovere**, a steel-making centre with ancient origins, dominates the northern lake. The town has an historic quarter, an art gallery (the Accademia di Belle Arti Tadini Gallery; <www.accademiatadini.it>) and a café-lined lakefront where the first steamer was launched on the lake in 1841. At **Pisogne**, across the water, the church of Santa Maria delle Neve is known as La Cappella Sistina dei Poveri (the Poor Man's Sistine Chapel) on account of the beautiful fresco cycle (1534) by Romanino.

From Pisogne you can drive north through the **Camonica Valley**, named after the Bronze-Age Camuni tribe who recorded scenes of everyday life by carving on the rocks of the valley floor. The valley is nowadays marred by industry but the rock engravings, which span several thousand years from the Ice Age to the Roman era, constitute one of the largest and finest collections of prehistoric art in Europe. The engravings are scattered all along the valley but the best examples are contained within Capo di Ponte's **Parco Nazionale delle Incisioni Rupestri** (National Park of Rock Engravings).

South of Lake Iseo lies the hilly, wine-producing region of **Franciacorta**. The Strada del Vino Franciacorta (<www.strada delfranciacorta.it>) is an 80-km (50-mile) wine route from Brescia to Lake Iseo, featuring vineyard tours and tastings. Franciacorta produces red and white wines but is best known for *spumante*, made according to Champagne methods.

LOMBARD CITIES

Bergamo

Following the Napoleonic army on horseback in 1800, Stendhal arrived in Bergamo from Milan having crossed 'the loveliest country in the world'. Today the *autostrada* and a great swathe of industry separate the cities, but Bergamo itself has seen remarkably little change over the two centuries. The modern city was constructed on the plain in the late 19th and early 20th century, but the Città Alta, the hilltop city where Stendhal stayed, is one of Italy's most alluring medieval centres.

From the Città Bassa, the pleasant enough but traffic-filled Lower City, a cable car takes you 100m (330ft) up the hill – and 500 years back in time. In 1428 Bergamo was swallowed up by the Venetian Republic; the great walls encircling the upper city, the fortress and the lions of St Mark all bear witness to over three and a half centuries under the sway of the Serenissima.

The bustling streets of Bergamo's Città Alta

Piazza Vecchia

Via Gombito and Via Colleoni, lively medieval streets lined by delectable little food shops and eateries, lead from the upper cable-car terminal to the heart of old Bergamo. The enchanting

The Contarini fountain and Palazzo Nuovo in Piazza Vecchia

Piazza Vecchia is a showpiece of medieval and Renaissance buildings, surrounding the beautiful Contarini fountain. On the southern side of the square the magnificent Venetian-Gothic **Palazzo Ragione** is the oldest communal palace in Italy, built in the 12th century though much remodelled. The elegant external stairway leads up to the main hall (open at weekends and for exhibitions) which houses a collection of fresco panels taken from nearby churches and convents. The Torre Civica, known more familiarly as the **Campanone**, is the city's bell tower which still chimes 100 times every evening at 10pm, in memory of the curfew under the Venetians. On the far side of the piazza the imposing white building is the Palazzo Nuovo, which today serves as the civic library.

Piazza del Duomo
Beyond Piazza Vecchia's loggia lies the smaller **Piazza del Duomo**, which is crammed with three major monuments.

The **Cappella Colleoni** (open Mar–Oct Tues–Sun 9am–12.30pm, 2–6.30pm, Nov–Feb 9am–12.30pm, 2–4.30pm) was built in 1472–6 as a mausoleum for the Venetian *condottiere* (mercenary), Bartolomeo Colleoni, who had the old sacristy of the neighbouring Santa Maria Maggiore demolished to create the space. A masterpiece of the early Lombard Renaissance, it has a multicoloured marble facade enriched by medallions, columns, sculpture and reliefs. The interior is no less opulent, decorated by Tiepolo frescoes and containing the intricately carved tomb of Colleoni, surmounted by a gold equestrian statue of the *condottiere*. The chapel also contains the tomb of his daughter, Medea, who predeceased him.

The adjoining church of **Santa Maria Maggiore** (open Mon–Sat 9am–12.30pm, 2.30–6pm, Sun 9am–1pm, 3–6pm) has a beautiful Gothic porch adorned with statues and reliefs. The interior was reconstructed in the 16th century and has a profusion of gilt, stuccowork and paintings as well as some fine Florentine and Flemish tapestries and exquisite inlaid panels on the (roped-off) choir stalls, designed by Lorenzo Lotto. Back in the piazza, the charming octagonal **Baptistery** is a copy of the 14th-century original which used to be inside the basilica. The **Duomo** (currently closed for restoration) is the poor relation in a remarkable group of buildings, its late 19th-century facade looking somewhat sober beside that of Santa Maria Maggiore and the Cappella Colleoni.

Off Via Gombito, the Via Solata leads up to **La Rocca**,

Santa Maria Maggiore

The composer Gaetano Donizetti, one of the great masters of bel-canto opera, was born in Bergamo in 1797. He is commemorated in the city by a street, a theatre, a memorial, a monument and the Museo Donizettiano. He was a highly successful musician but endured great tragedy in his personal life. All three of his children died at a young age and his wife succumbed to the plague. Donizetti suffered from syphilis, was institionalised, and died in Bergamo in 1848.

a 14th-century fortress that was reconstructed by the Venetians. This commands fine views across the city and is home to the History Museum, dedicated to the Risorgimento. The Natural History Museum and the Archaeological Museum can be found at the **Cittadella** to the south, built as a fortress by Bernabò Visconti though much altered and restored over the centuries.

The cultural highlight of the Città Bassa is the **Galleria Accademia Carrara**, (Piazza Giacomo Carrara 82; open Tues–Sun 10am–1pm, 2.30–5.30pm; admission fee; <www.accademiacarrara.bergamo.it>), a rich collection of 15th–18th-century art, and particularly strong on the Venetian and Lombard schools. Artists include Pisanello, the Bellinis, Mantegna, Carpaccio, Botticelli, Raphael, Titian, Tintoretto and Lorenzo Lotto.

Brescia

Lombardy's second city after Milan, industrial **Brescia** lacks the charm (and the tourists) of Bergamo or Verona. You are unlikely to choose it as a base, but for those interested in art and architecture, there is an outstanding museum complex and some fine monuments reflecting the various eras of its long history. The town flourished under the Romans, who left their mark in the grid layout of the city and the Capitoline Temple. In medieval times the town became a wealthy independent commune, supplying arms and armour to Europe; but like Bergamo, it came under Venetian rule from 1426–1797.

Piazza della Loggia

Life centres on three very different squares at the centre of the city. The most appealing is the Venetian-style **Piazza della Loggia**, the loggia being the richly decorated palazzo dominating the square – today the town hall. The upper level was designed by the leading Venetian architects Palladio and Sansovino. On the south side the piazza is flanked by the Monte Vecchio di Pietà (1489) and the Monte Nuovo di Pietà (late-16th century), the old and the new pawnbrokers; on the opposite side of the square the Torre dell'Orologio echoes St Mark's Torre dell'Orologio in Venice, with a splendid astronomical clock (1544) and two clockwork figures that strike the hour. Neighbouring **Piazza della Vittoria**,

Brescia's Palazzo Publico in the Piazza della Loggia

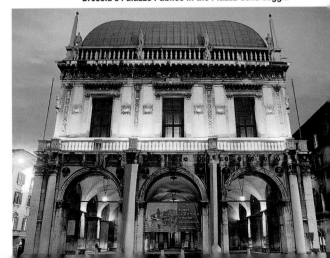

The Duomo Nuovo and Rotonda

accessed via an archway, was built during the Mussolini era and couldn't be more of a contrast.

Piazza Paolo VI

The religious core of the city is **Piazza Paolo VI**, formerly the Piazza del Duomo. The square changed its name in honour of Pope Paul VI (1897–1978) who was born in Brescia. The massive **Duomo Nuovo** (New Cathedral; open Mon–Sat 7.30am–noon, 4–7pm), whose huge green cupola can be spotted from afar, stunts the lovely **Rotonda**, the Duomo Vecchio or Old Cathedral. This is an unusual round Romanesque building constructed on the site of an 8th-century basilica which was destroyed by fire in 1097. The interior contains the beautifully decorated sarcophagus of Bishop Berardo Maggi (1308) in red Verona marble. The austere building with a tower to the left of the Duomo Nuovo is the Broletto, the medieval town hall, today the city council offices.

Roman Ruins and Museo della Città

The Via dei Musei beside the Broletto takes you to the **Piazza del Foro**, the old Roman forum. Towering above it are the mighty columns of the Capitoline Temple erected in AD73 by Emperor Vespasian. Beside the temple the **Roman Theatre** is currently undergoing excavation. Archaeological finds from the site are housed in the nearby **Museo della Città** (City Museum; open Tues–Sun 10am–5.30pm; admission fee), laid out in the monastery of Santa Giulia. Founded in AD753 by the Lombard king, Desiderius, the complex was continually extended up until the Renaissance and features the Romanesque church of Santa Maria in Solario, rich in frescoes and home to the rare, bejewelled 9th-century Cross of Desiderius, and the medieval Basilica of San Salvatore whose Nun's Choir is decorated with striking early 15th-century frescoes. The museum explores some 2,000 years of the city's history (from prehistory to the Venetian era), through statuary, frescoes, mosaics, medieval graves and other works of art. From the Roman era, the highlight is the bronze life-sized statue of *The Winged Victory*, discovered in the Capitoline Temple in 1826. In addition to the permanent displays, the museum hosts major art exhibitions (<www.lineadombra.it>).

Ceiling of Santa Maria in Solario in the Museo della Città

Rising above the forum is the vast 14th-century Visconti **Castello** (open daily 8am–8pm), incorporating the Museum of the Risorgimento and the Museum of Ancient Arms. Due south of the Piazza del Foro, the **Pinacoteca Tosio-Martinengo** (Piazza

Stradivarius statue in Cremona

Moretto; open Tues–Sun Jun–Sep 10am–5pm, Oct–May 9.30am–1pm, 2.30–5pm) has a fine collection of works by Brescian Renaissance and baroque masters who were deeply influenced by the Venetian school.

Cremona

Synonymous with Stradivarius, **Cremona** has been the centre of the violin-making industry since the 16th century. Andrea Amati created the first modern violin here in 1566 and his more famous pupil, Antonio Stradivarius, was born here in 1644. The International School of Violin Making ensures the continuation of the tradition and concerts often take place in the town. The International Festival of Stringed Instruments takes place every third October.

Music apart, Cremona is a provincial market town on the River Po, with a fine medieval square but not a great deal else to detain you. The city's main monuments are all grouped on the **Piazza del Comune**. The magnificent **Duomo** facade incorporates elements of the Romanesque, Gothic and Renaissance styles; inside (open daily 7.30am–noon, 3.30–7pm) the nave and chancel are decorated with frescoes. The **Torrazzo**, at 113m (370ft), is the tallest bell tower in Italy – the energetic can climb 487 steps to the top for fine views over the city. To the right of the Duomo the octagonal baptistery was built at the same time and remodelled in Renaissance style. Across from the Duomo, the red-brick Loggia dei Militii was the former headquarters of the local militia; the Palazzo del Comune, the town hall, is home to the **Civica Collezione**

di Violini (open Mon–Sat 9am–6pm, Sun 10am–6pm, Nov–Mar closed Mon; admission fee; guided tours only). This tiny collection of historic violins includes Stradivarius' Cremonese 1715. You can hear these rare instruments played on a Monday or Saturday at 11.15am and noon (also 3.30pm in summer) providing there are at least 15 other visitors (tel: 0372 22138 for information). More Stradivarian memorabilia can be seen at the Museo Stradivariano within the Museu Civico Ala Ponzone (Via Ugolani Dati 4), 10 minutes' walk north of the Piazza del Comune.

Mantua

Formerly one of the great Renaissance courts in Europe, **Mantua** (or Mantova) is nowadays a provincial town with unprepossessing outskirts and a diminished population. But it has a lovely unspoilt medieval centre concentrated around

Sunset over Mantua

Canal reflections

three interlinked piazzas. The vast Palazzo Ducale, the Palazzo Tè and other great architectural monuments of Mantua are testimony to the power and artistic patronage of the Gonzaga family who lorded it over the town for nearly four centuries.

Palazzo Ducale

The huge cobbled **Piazza Sordello** is dominated by the **Palazzo Ducale** (open Tues–Sun 8.45am–7.15pm; admission fee; tel: 0376 352100 for information, 041 2411897 for tickets; <www.mantovaducale.it>). From March to October reservations must be made in advance to see the Camera degli Sposa where only 1,500 visitors are permitted daily). The palazzo was originally built by the despotic Bonacolsi, lords of Mantua from 1272–1328. When the Gonzagas took control of the town in 1328, the palace became their fortress and home, and was extended over the centuries to become a colossal complex of over 450 rooms, with courtyards, piazzas and gardens. Although much altered, the palace still gives a vivid idea of the brilliance of the Gonzaga Court.

Among the artistic highlights are Pisanello's unfinished series of 15th-century frescoes of the *Knights of the Round Table*, 16th-century Flemish tapestries modelled on Raphael's cartoons of the *Acts of the Apostles*, Rubens' huge portrait of *The Gonzagas Adoring the Holy Trinity*, and most famous of all, the **Camera degli Sposi** (Bridal Chamber) in the Castello di San Giorgio, decorated by Mantegna's frescoes (1465–74), glorifying the Gonzaga family. A spectacular experiment of perspectival illusionism, the frescoes cover the entire room, including the architectural features. Most innovative of all is the trompe-l'oeil ceiling, with putti and ladies in waiting peering down over the foreshortened balustrade.

Piazza Broletto and Piazza delle Erbe

From Piazza Sordello an archway leads to **Piazza Broletto**, the centre of medieval public life. The red-brick Broletto is the old town hall which separates the square from Piazza delle Erbe. On the Piazza Sordello side the Torre della Gabbia was converted to a prison and has an iron cage where prisoners were put on public display.

Named after the fruit and vegetable market, the **Piazza delle Erbe** is the loveliest of Mantua's squares. It is framed on three sides by porticoes and shops, and at night you can dine out by candlelight in front of the arcades of the Palazzo della Ragione. This large 13th-century, crenellated palace hosts major art exhibitions. Below piazza level stands the beautiful Romanesque (though remodelled) **Rotonda di San Lorenzo** (open Mon–Fri 10am–1pm, 2–6pm, Sat and Sun 10am–6pm), the oldest of Mantua's churches. The interior walls and vaults still preserve traces of Byzantine-influenced frescoes.

A quiet Mantuan sidestreet

Mantua's most famous sons are the poet Virgil, whose statue you can see in a niche on Palazzo Broletto, and Andrea Mantegna, who was court painter to the Gonzagas and produced the famous Camera degli Sposi in the Palazzo Ducale.

Basilica di Sant'Andrea

Situated on the neighbouring Piazza Mantegna, the **Basilica di Sant'Andrea** (open daily 8am–noon, 3–7pm) was a major landmark in Renaissance architecture. Replacing a Romanesque church, it was designed by the great Florentine architect and theorist Leon Battista Alberti for Lodovico Il Gonzaga. Inspired by classical architecture and evoking the grandeur of ancient Rome, the basilica combines a temple front and triumphal arch. The imposing interior is laid out on a Roman basilica plan and profusely decorated. The first chapel on the left houses the tomb of the painter, Andrea Mantegna, who died in Mantua in 1506.

Palazzo Tè

A bus ride or 20-minute walk from the centre will bring you to **Palazzo Tè** (open Tues–Sun 9am–6pm, Mon 1–6pm; admission fee). This exuberant villa was built and decorated in the mannerist style by the architect and painter Giulio Romano (1499–1546) for the pleasure-loving Federico II Gonzaga and his mistress, Isabella Boschetti. Fantastic frescoes adorn the rooms, ranging from the life-size horses of the Gonzagas to the erotic murals of the Sala di Amore e Psyche (Cupid and Psyche Room). The tour de force is the Sala dei Giganti (Room of the Giants) depicting the victory of Jupiter over the rebellious Titans. The entire room, including the vaulted ceiling, is frescoed to give an illusionistic effect, with rocks tumbling down on to the Titans (and seemingly the spectators too).

Gladiators once fought, now opera singers perform, in Verona's arena

VERONA

Verona is a city of superlatives: the largest and most enticing city in the Veneto after Venice, boasting the world's third-largest Roman amphitheatre, some of the finest piazzas and monuments in northern Italy, along with the grandest open-air opera. Above all, however, Verona is celebrated for Shakespearean tales of young love. Crowds from all corners of the world come to pay respects to the so-called Casa di Giuletta (Juliet's House) and the famous marble balcony.

Strategically placed on the River Adige at a crossing of major trade routes, the town flourished under Roman rule, but it was under the hugely powerful and frequently tyrannical Scaligeri (or della Scala) dynasty (1260–1387) that the city reached its zenith. The Visconti from Milan had a brief spell as lords of Verona; but from 1405 the city came under the sway of the Venetians, who ruled here until the French invasion of 1796.

Piazza Brà and the Arena

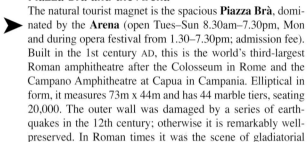

The natural tourist magnet is the spacious **Piazza Brà**, dominated by the **Arena** (open Tues–Sun 8.30am–7.30pm, Mon and during opera festival from 1.30–7.30pm; admission fee). Built in the 1st century AD, this is the world's third-largest Roman amphitheatre after the Colosseum in Rome and the Campano Amphitheatre at Capua in Campania. Elliptical in form, it measures 73m x 44m and has 44 marble tiers, seating 20,000. The outer wall was damaged by a series of earthquakes in the 12th century; otherwise it is remarkably well-preserved. In Roman times it was the scene of gladiatorial combat, mock battles and games; today it is the stage for the world-famous Verona opera performances *(see box below)*.

Visiting Verona

Verona may be steeped in history, but the heart of the city is very much alive, especially during the opera season. Tourists mainly visit on fleeting half-day tours, but this is a city which merits at least a one-night stay to take in the wealth of sights – and ideally the opera too. Nearly all of the city's attractions are found in the historic quarter, and can easily be covered on foot. The streets of the centre are largely traffic-free and the city lends itself to strolling. The excellent-value VeronaCard, valid for a day or week (€8 and €12) allows unlimited travel on city buses and admissions to museums, monuments and churches.

You don't have to be an opera buff to enjoy a performance in Verona's arena. The open-air experience in one of the world's great Roman amphitheatres is an unforgettable one – even if you can't understand a word. The mood is festive and fun rather than formal. You can take your own food (alcohol is not allowed but there are vendors selling wine). The programme features favourite operas, typically Aida, Carmen and Tosca, and the performances are lavish affairs. *(See page 87 for details).*

On the west side of the square, the gently curving Listone is lined by open-air cafés, pizzerias and restaurants, a popular rendezvous and favourite spot to watch the leisurely *passeggiata* (evening stroll) and street-theatre performers.

Venetian lion, Piazza delle Erbe

Piazza delle Erbe

From the Listone, the elegant, shop-lined Via Mazzini brings you into bustling **Piazza delle Erbe**, the heart of Verona and formerly the Roman forum. The market nowadays is more a source of snacks and souvenirs than herbs or fresh produce, but it is still an appealing piazza with its white canopies, handsome *palazzi*, marble fountain and monuments. Finest of the palaces is the baroque Palazzo Maffei, surmounted by six statues of Roman gods and flanked by the Gardello Tower (1370). On the west side is the over-restored crenellated Casa dei Mercanti (14th century); across the square the much-restored Casa Mazzanti was built for the Scaligeri family and decorated with 16th-century frescoes. On the same side is the Domus Nova (1659) and the Palazzo della Ragione (Palace of Justice, *see page 78*).

Piazza dei Signori and Arche Scaligere

Linking Piazza dei Signori with Piazza delle Erbe is the Arco della Costa, 'arch of the rib' – the rib referring to the whalebone hanging below the arch, which – according to legend – will fall on the first honest person to pass underneath. Centre

Juliet's Club was set up to sustain the myth of Romeo and Juliet and the romantic image of Verona. Thousands of unsolicited letters arrive each year, from all over the world, addressed to the Shakespearean heroine. These are all read and each one is answered by one of the many volunteer Juliet secretaries. If you want to add to the fan mail visit <www.julietclub.com>.

of civic life until the 16th century, the **Piazza dei Signori** is a far more formal square than Piazza delle Erbe, reminiscent of a stage set from a Shakespeare play. The trio of civic buildings are the **Palazzo della Ragione** (also called Palazzo del Comune), the Palazzo del Governo, and – most elegant of all – the Venetian Renaissance **Loggia del Consiglio**, topped by five statues of famous Romans. The Palazzo della Ragione, with a pretty courtyard and Gothic stairway, is currently undergoing a major conversion to a multipurpose exhibition centre. A statue of a characteristically gloomy-looking Dante takes centre stage. The poet spent time in exile in Verona as a guest of Bartolomeo I della Scala.

Beyond the arch lies the little Romanesque church of Santa Maria Antica and the **Arche Scaligere**, the extraordinary Gothic mausoleums of the Scaligeri family. These are so lofty it is difficult to see any detail – though you can spot the Scaligeri symbol of the five-rung ladder *(scala)* on the palisade that surrounds them. The most conspicuous is the equestrian tomb of Cangrande ('The Big Dog') which is a copy of the original, now in Verona's Castelvecchio *(see page 81)*.

La Casa di Giuletta

There is no evidence that the **Casa di Giuletta** was Juliet's house – or even that Romeo and Juliet existed. The medieval dwelling was acquired by the city of Verona in 1907 and the famous balcony (which is far too high anyway for Romeo to have climbed) was added in 1935. Nevertheless Shakespeare fans and romantics flock here to gaze at the tiny courtyard and marble balcony. The walls have been cleaned of graffiti and Juliet pilgrims are now requested to leave their love messages on the board inside the entrance arcade, in the mailbox or on the Juliet website *(see box opposite)*. The bronze statue of Juliet is a focus of attention, particularly the gleaming right breast (rubbing it is said to bring you luck in love). The house interior (open Tues–Sun 8.30am–7.30pm, Mon 1.30–7.30pm; admission fee) feels far from medieval but enables visitors to pose on the balcony. Romeo and Juliet Verona tours also include 'Juliet's Tomb' in a Franciscan monastery 800m (775 yards) south of Piazza Brà. Fans from around the world get married here in civil ceremonies.

Romeo, Romeo...

Churches and Roman Theatre

South of the Casa di Giulietta is **San Fermo Maggiore** (open Mon–Sat 10am–6pm, Sun 1–6pm, winter Sun only 1.30–5pm; admission fee), a beautiful Romanesque church which was reconstructed in the 14th century. The interior has a wealth of frescoes and a magnificent Gothic ship's-keel roof. Don't miss the Romanesque Chiesa Inferiore (Lower Church) over which the main church was built and which today serves as a crypt.

Northeast of Piazza dei Signori is **Sant'Anastasia** (open Mon–Sat 9am–6pm, Sun 1–6pm, winter Tues–Sat 1.30–4pm, Sun 1–5pm; admission fee), the largest church in Verona,

Verona's Duomo

with a soaring Gothic interior and vast red marble pillars dividing the aisles. Among the many frescoes is Pisanello's *St George and the Princess* (1433–8) above the arch of the Pellegrini Chapel to the right of the altar. To the northwest, near the river, is the Romanesque/Gothic **Duomo** (open Mon–Sat 10am–5.30pm, Sun 1.30–5.30pm, winter Tues–Sat 10am–1pm, Sun 1–5pm; admission fee), which has a finely carved portal and, inside, an *Assumption* (1530) by Titian (first chapel to the left of the main entrance). More charming than the actual Duomo is the ancient little San Giovanni in Fonte, originally the baptistery, and the Church of St Elena, both accessed through the door below the Duomo's organ.

Across the river lie the ruins of the **Roman Theatre** (open Tues–Sun 8.30am–7pm, Mon 1.30–7pm; admission fee) With beautiful views of the city, this provides a fine setting in summer for the Shakespeare Festival, concerts, ballet and jazz *(see page 88)*. From here you can take a lift up to the monastery where exhibits from the small Archaeological Museum are displayed.

Castelvecchio and San Zeno Maggiore

In the 1350s, Cangrande II della Scala built the **Castelvecchio** beside the Adige River as a fortress and residence. The triple-arched Ponte Scaligeri (rebuilt after destruction in World War II) was constructed across the river here as a private bridge and an escape route in the event of enemy attacks or local rebellions. The Castelvecchio has been beautifully converted to the **Museo d'Arte** (Art Museum; open Tues–Sun 8.30am–7.30pm, Mon 1.45–7.30pm; admission fee). The collection includes some fine examples of medieval sculpture as well as paintings by Carpaccio, the Bellinis, Mantegna, Tiepolo and other Venetian masters.

A walk westwards along the river bank from Castelvecchio will take you in the direction of **San Zeno Maggiore** (open Mon–Sat 8.30am–6pm, Sun 1–6pm, winter Sun only 1–5pm; admission fee), arguably the finest Romanesque church in northern Italy. San Zeno, a 4th-century saint, built the original church on this site, and his tomb lies in the crypt along with those of other saints and bishops. The facade is beautifully proportioned and features a rose window representing the wheel of fortune, a main portal with marble bas-reliefs and wooden doors with 48 superb bronze panels of biblical scenes. The interior is spacious and simple, with Andrea Mantegna's exquisite triptych, *Madonna and Saints* (1459) on the high altar.

WHAT TO DO

SPORTS AND OUTDOOR ACTIVITIES

The lakes are a sporting paradise. You can choose from a huge range of aquatic sports, trekking in the hinterland, mountain biking, horse riding, golf or – for the more adventurous – paragliding, hang-gliding and canyoning

Watersports

Lake Garda is a mecca for sailors and windsurfers, particularly in the north where the lake narrows and the winds create ideal conditions all year round; Sirmione in the south is another good spot for windsurfing. The resorts of Riva del Garda and Torbole have numerous watersports schools with gear to rent and tuition for all levels. Gargnano hosts the annual Centomiglia sailing regatta in early September. Lake Como has sailing, windsurfing and water-skiing; you can hire motorboats from Como, and some main resorts such as Bellagio and Menaggio have beaches, pools and water sports.

Swimming. There are a number of great places to swim in the lakes, particularly Lake Garda, which has the cleanest and warmest waters of the three main lakes. Some resorts provide lidos with beaches, pools and water sports; others have just a narrow strip of shingle. The waters around the town of Como are polluted but as you go further north the lake becomes much cleaner.

Hiking, Climbing and Cable Cars

Trekkers are increasingly attracted by the quiet routes and breathtaking views above the lakes. The ridges and Alpine

Water taxis and Isola di San Giulio, Lake Orta

Tour boat guide

foothills offer some wonderful walking, from easy lake or woodland trails to strenuous climbs in the mountains. The Club Alpino Italiano (Italian Alpine Club, Via Petrella 19, 20124 Milan, tel: 02 2057231, <www.cai milano.it>) organizes guided tours and runs refuges along the mountain itineraries. The best months for walks in the Alps are May to October.

For those who want the views without the hike, there are some spectacular cable-cars trips including Malcesine to Monte Baldo, Stresa to Monte Mottarone and Como to Brunate. Beware however, that the summer haze frequently restricts the vistas.

As well as stunning views, the Monte Baldo ridge on Lake Garda, accessed from Malcesine by cable car, offers opportunities for mountaineering, hang-gliding, free climbing and canyoning, from amateur to competitive level. Further north around Torbole and Riva del Garda free climbers hang above the lake. Above Lake Como the peaks of the Grigna and Resogone are for serious hikers, and there is free climbing at Lecco.

Cycling and Mountain Biking

The locals are keen cyclists and cycle paths are being created around the lakes, especially Maggiore and Garda. Mountain biking is particularly popular, especially on Monte Baldo and the northern end of Lake Garda, the hills and mountains around Lake Como and Mottarone above Stresa on Lake Maggiore. In summer the ski slopes make natural trails for mountain biking, cycling and hiking. Mountain-biking itineraries are supplied by local tourist offices, bikes and helmets can be hired and guides are also available. Varese will host the Road Cycling World Championships in 2008.

Golf

Golf courses are dotted around the region, many of them with wonderful views of the lakes and Alps. The region around lakes Como and Maggiore has the best choice. One of the most prestigious and challenging courses is the Villa D'Este Golf Club near Montorfano, southeast of Como.

Spectator Sports

The Italian Grand Prix takes place in early September at Monza, 15km (9 miles) northeast of Milan. Soccer, as in the rest of Italy, is hugely popular, and especially since the Italian victory in the 2006 World Cup. The rival Milan clubs,

Lake Trips by Boat

Hopping on ferries is a great way of seeing the lakes. The first steamboats were launched in 1826; nowadays you can travel on hydrofoils (*aliscafi*), excursion cruisers, car ferries (*traghetti*) as well as the reasonably priced *battelli* (passenger ferryboats) which link up the towns and villages. Timetables are widely available from ticket offices and tourist information offices. Ferries run throughout the year though services are limited off-season. Drinks and snacks are usually available on board, and some ferries operating longer routes offer a three-course set lunch on board. On lakes Maggiore, Como and Garda, ferries are operated by Navigazione Laghi (visit <www.navlaghi.it> for maps and timetables). On the larger lakes, no single pass covers the entire lake, but the area is divided into zones for which you can purchase a 24-hour pass.

AC Milan and Inter play at the San Siro Stadium, Via Piccolomini 5, 5.5km (3½ miles) from the centre of Milan. Tickets can be booked through the AC and Inter websites on <www.acmilan.com> and <www.inter.it>.

Other Sports

Lombardy has 110 peaks exceeding 3,000m (9,840ft) and 600km (373 miles) of ski slopes. In the winter months it's possible to ski and snowboard at Monte Baldo (Lake Garda), Mottarone (Lake Maggiore), the Grigna mountains above Lecco (Lake Como) and the resorts above Bergamo and Brescia, but you can't always guarantee the snow. For information on ski resorts consult <www.skiinfo.it>. There are plenty of opportunities for horse riding in the hills and valleys and along the ridges. Equestrian centres offer lessons for all standards, as well as one- or two-day horse-riding tours.

ENTERTAINMENT

Most of the towns and villages on the lakes are peaceful places where visitors are content with a stroll and a drink or two in a lakeside bar or café. Lake Garda generally attracts a younger crowd and is the liveliest of the lakes, particularly Desenzano in the south, with bars, live music and around half a dozen nightclubs in and around the resort. Bardolino, on the other side of the lake, is quite a lively spot with plenty of bars open late as well as a couple of discos.

The larger towns in the region have bars with occasional live music, a jazz club or two, wine bars and discos which are often on the town outskirts. **Brescia**, a university city, is lively after dark especially on weekends. You can wine and dine at one of the many restaurants and wine bars in the piazzas and streets of the old town, enjoy concerts and opera at the Teatro Grande, live it up at late-night bars or just wander up to the castle to enjoy the views and an *aperitivo* on a café terrace.

Verona is famous for its Arena where opera extravaganzas are staged from late June to the end of August. Performances alternate, so that during one month you have a choice of at least four operas. Book well in advance – you can do so online at <www.arena.it> or by telephoning the call centre on 045 8005151. The Arena's website gives the full programme and a detailed seating plan. Seats range from the most expensive stalls (€160) to the unreserved stone steps up in the gods (€12). Only full-priced tickets can be purchased online. Reduced tickets can be obtained by telephoning the call centre or by visiting the ticket office in Via Dietro Anfiteatro, 6/b.

Hotels in the city get booked up well in advance for this period, so it is well worth checking that accommodation is available before reserving seats – you can do so on the Verona booking office at <www.veronapass.com>. An alter-

An opera performance in Verona's arena

native is to stay on the Verona side of Lake Garda and either drive or take a late public bus back from Verona to the lake.

At the same time as the operas, Verona's Roman Theatre stages the open-air **Shakespeare Festival** (with occasional performances in English), as well as concerts, ballet and jazz performances. For details and to book online visit <www.estate teatraleveronese.it>. Last-minute tickets are sold shortly before the performances. Free concerts are held regularly in the Piazza dei Signori during the summer months. Verona is also a great place for eating out, with numerous restaurants ranging from simple little trattorias to temples of gastronomy. The Listone on Piazza Bra, overlooking the Arena, is a lovely spot either for a pre- or post-prandial drink, *gelato* or full meal.

Stresa's **Settimane Musicali di Stresa** (<www.stresa.net/ settimanemusicale>) is an annual festival of classical concerts, performed by internationally renowned artists. The venues are churches, castles and villas located around Lake Maggiore and Lake Orta, and on the Borromeo Islands.

Aperitivi

The pre-prandial *aperitivo*, from around 6–9pm, is a way of life. The price of the drink may seem steep, but snacks, canapés and sometimes a whole buffet is included in the price and can provide a cheap alternative to dinner in a restaurant. Happy hour (two drinks for the price of one) is usually 7–9pm or 8–10pm. Some bars turn into discos at around 11pm or midnight. Cafés and bars offer a remarkable range of beverages: Prosecco or *spumante* (Italian sparkling wine, which you can have by the glass), *pirlo* (white wine with Campari or Aperol), Negroni (Campari with vermouth and gin) and a long list of liqueurs and other cocktails. An *enoteca* or wine bar will have a huge list of vintage and non-vintage bottles, with snacks or sometimes main courses to go with them.

An atmospheric shopping arcade in Bellagio

SHOPPING

Northern Italians demand style and elegance and this is reflected in the shops in cities such as Brescia, Bergamo and Verona. Lakeside villages and resorts are more limited but the larger among them have some stylish fashions, and plenty of shops selling gourmet food, olive oil and wine.

Fashions

Serious fashion followers will head for nearby **Milan**, trend-setting capital of Italy (for details see *Berlitz Pocket Guide Milan*). But there are other cities in the region offering a stylish selection of fashions, leather and jewellery. **Verona** is an appealing place to shop, especially the traffic-free Via Mazzini in the centre with its designer (and other) boutiques. The street is also home to Fiorucci, the city's largest department store selling the latest fashions in casual wear and accessories. **Brescia** is another good shopping city, with well-known designer stores, jewellery shops, antiques and art galleries. Close to Brescia the **Franciacorta Outlet Village** in Rodengo Saiano (7km/4½ miles west of Brescia, Ospitaletto exit off the A4 motorway; open May–Sep Mon–Fri 10am–8pm, Sat–Sun 10am–9pm, Oct–April daily 10am-8pm; <www.franciacorta outlet.it>) has 155 stores selling clothing, shoes, accessories, cosmetics, household items, linens and electrical goods. The streets of **Bergamo**'s Città Bassa (Lower Town), especially Il Sentierone and Via XX Settembre, offer a wide choice of fashions, leather goods and jewellery. La Rinascente on Via XX Settembre is an up-market department store selling stylish fashions for men and women, along with cosmetics, accessories and household goods.

Silk ties in every colour

Como is famous for high-quality silk. The tourist office there has a list of silk factory outlets in the area where you can get 40–70 percent discounts on silk prints, scarves, ties, and shirts which are produced for the top designers. Montero, a leading designer and producer of luxury silk, has opened a new store called La Tessitura at Via Roosevelt 2/a, Como (open daily; tel: 031 321666, <www.latessi tura.com>) within a spectacularly converted late-19th century factory. Textiles and accessories include jacquard silks, bags, knitware and belts created from vintage ties. Frey Emporio della Seta has an outlet at Via Risorgimento 49 in Fino Mornasco (tel: 031 927538) and shops in Como at Via Boldoni and Via Garibaldi. The Spaccio Ratti at Villa Sucota, Via Cernobbio 17, Como (tel: 031 233262) sells designer ties, scarves, shawls, and shirts from a lakeside villa; their larger outlet at Via Madonna 32 in Guanzate (11km/7 miles southwest of Como; tel: 031 576000) has a wider selection.

Locally designed and produced garments

Markets

Watch out for the local weekly or fortnightly markets in the larger towns where you can pick up anything from fashions and handbags to whole hams and cheeses. The largest market in the region is at **Luino** on Lake Maggiore's eastern shore, which claims to be the biggest weekly market in Europe. There are some 350 stalls, attracting bargain hunters from Switzerland, Austria and Germany – as well as Italy. Some of the main towns host monthly antiques markets where you can browse among handicrafts, worthless junk or genuine antiques. **Brescia**'s Mercatino dell'Antiquariato, held in the Piazza della Vittoria on the second weekend of the month, is one of the best. Look out for the work of goldsmiths, engravers and wrought-iron artisans in Bergamo and Brescia, and ceramicists around Mantua. Local tourist offices can supply you with details of markets and any food and wine fairs that are coming to the region. Bargaining at any of the markets is always worth a try, however limited your Italian.

Food and Wine

Lakeside villages and resorts teem with tiny delis selling everything from home-cured hams, speciality risotto rice, herbs and honey to local wines, grappa and liqueurs. The best olive oil in the region is made around Lake Garda, a pale aromatic oil. The panettone Christmas cake, made with raisins and candied orange and lemon zest, is a Milanese speciality; nowadays it's sold all year round throughout Italy and abroad. Cremona is known for *torrone*, Italy's version of nougat, and *mostardo di Cremona*, which is pickled fruits in mustard oil. Local wines are often a good buy, whether it's the reds from Bardolino (Lake Garda) or Valtellina (near Lake Como) or the sparkling whites from Franciacorta (Lake Iseo). Tourist offices can supply details of wine tours, estates and cellars.

Bergamo's medieval Città Alta (Upper City) is delightful for shopping, its medieval Via Gombito lined by groceries selling tempting local produce and some stylish little boutiques. A regular bus service links both the upper and lower town of Bergamo with Orio del Serio airport just 5km (3 miles) away, making it ideal for last-minute shopping. If you don't make it to the town you can always stock

---

Torrone from Cremona

Legend has it that at their sumptuous wedding feast in 1441 Bianca Maria Visconti and Francesco Sforza were presented with a magnificent dessert in the shape of Cremona's belltower (known as the Torrione). Made of egg whites, honey and nuts, it was named after the tower and presented to courts throughout Europe. Modern *torrone* is a popular confectionary like nougat, usually made industrially and sold throughout Italy and beyond. A few artisans do however remain faithful to the old recipes. Cremona still clings to the *torrone* culture — and every October hosts a *torrone* festival.

up at **Agripromo** at the airport (<www.agripromo.it>) which specializes in authentic local produce (salami, cheeses, polenta della Bergamasca, olive oil and Valcalepio wines). The shop also has a branch in Bergamo at Via Borgo Palazzo 128. A cheaper option is the hypermarket in the OrioCenter across the road from the airport, which is Europe's largest shopping centre (<www.oriocenter.it>).

Mountain cheese, Luino market

CHILDREN

Although the lakes cater more for adults than children, there is no shortage of activities for youngsters. Along with ferry and cable-cars rides there are pedaloes and rowing boats to hire, parks and medieval castles to visit, and on Lake Garda, the largest theme park in Italy. All the lakes have watersports tuition available and some resorts have sandy or pebble beaches or lidos equipped with pools.

Peschiera on Lake Garda is a children's paradise – not the town itself, but the stretch of shoreline to the north which has Italy's number-one theme park, **Gardaland** (at Castelnuovo 5km/3 miles north of Peschiera; open daily Apr–mid-June and mid–end Sep 10am–6pm, mid-June–mid-Sep 9.30am–midnight, weekend openings in winter; tel: 045 6449777, <www.gardaland.it>; admission fee, reduced charges after 8pm). The theme park boasts 40 attractions and 40 shows, aimed at both adults and children. Laser shows and fireworks add to the attractions on summer evenings. Be pre-

Fun at the fair in Pescheria

pared for very long queues in summer. Tickets can be booked online. Just to the north, **Canevaworld** (<www.canevaworld.it>; admission fee) comprises the Aqua Paradise water park (open mid-May–mid-Sep 10am–6pm, until 7pm July–Aug), Movieland Studios, with stage sets and special effects (open Apr–Sep 10am–6pm, until 7pm July–Aug, until 11pm Sat) and, evenings only, Medieval Times, featuring a tournament and banquet.

Acquasplash Franciacorta (at Corte Franca, near Lake Iseo, open daily 9.30am–7pm in summer; <www.acquasplash.it>, admission fee) offers plenty of aquatic activity with swimming pools, slides and chutes.

Parco della Villa Pallavicino *(see page 30)* at Stresa on Lake Maggiore is a popular spot for youngsters, with 40 different species of animals and birds, many of them roaming free in the park, and a well-equipped playground. In summer a little electric train links the park with central Stresa. On the other side of the lake **Rocca Borromeo** is one of the region's best-preserved castles, and home to a doll museum. *(see page 33)*. Lake Garda has several medieval castles.

Budding gladiators can let their imaginations run wild in Verona's beautifully preserved **Roman Arena**, and older children might enjoy one of the opera extravaganzas (this is not formal opera – you can sit on the steps up in the gods and take a picnic). For other ideas to keep kids amused in Verona visit <www.veronaforkids.it>.

Calendar of Events

There are numerous annual events around the lakes, from Verona's world-famous operas and Milan's fashion fairs to low-key food and wine festivals and local village events. Information is available from local tourist offices. The following is a selection of the highlights:

February/March: Carnival in Verona, Lecco and other towns and villages; parades, floats, music and dancing.

Early April: Celebrations at Pontida, Bergamo, to mark the 1176 defeat of Barbarossa by the Lombard League.

Easter: Parade of symbolic floats at Bormio near Sondrio and costumed parade at Schivenoglia, Mantova.

Last Sunday of May: Legnano's *Sagra del Carroccio*: medieval pageant and *palio* contest commemorating the 1176 Lombard League victory over Barbarossa.

June: International piano festival, Bergamo. Festival of San Giovanni Battista, 24 June, Isola Comacina, Lake Como; mass in the ruins of the basilica, candlelit boat procession and fireworks.

Late June–August: Verona's opera season at the Arena (<www.arena.it>) and the Shakespeare Festival at the Teatro Romano, Verona, with English-language performances by the Royal Shakespeare Company; also jazz, ballet and modern-dance performances (<www.estateteatraleveronese.it>).

July: International Sailing Regatta at Gargnano, Lake Garda. Third week: Lago Maggiore Jazz, performances at Stresa, Angera and other towns on Lake Maggiore, attracting big names in the world of jazz.

August: Illuminated boat race followed by fireworks at Laveno Mombello, near Varese.

August–September: Stresa's *Settimane Musicali*, festival of classical music. *Palio Baradello* at Como, celebrating the victory of Barbarossa over Milan.

September: Italian Grand Prix at Monza (first week). Music Festival in Ascona, Lake Maggiore. Como's international music festival (Sep–Nov). *Mostro Autunno Pavese*, gastronomic festival in Pavia. *Festa dell'Uva* (Grape Festival) on the last weekend of the month, Bardolino, Lake Garda. Franciacorta wine and food festival. Firework display, Sirmione, Lake Garda.

EATING OUT

Eating out is one of the great pleasures of a holiday in the lakes. Many of the restaurants enjoy seductive lakeside settings, and offer a wide choice of appetising dishes from smoked cured hams and seasoned sausages to creamy risottos, flavoursome pastas and fish fresh from the lake. Each region has its specialities: from Brescia comes *casonsei*, giant ravioli stuffed with parmesan, spinach and eggs; from Lake Iseo the highly prized baked *tinca* or tench, served with polenta; from Mantua, *tortelli di zucca*, delicate egg pasta enveloping pureed pumpkin; from Milan the famous *risotto alla milanese*, coloured and flavoured with saffron.

Rice, rather than pasta, is the mainstay of the local diet, grown on the vast paddy fields around the Po and in the

Harbourside restaurant, Lazise, Lake Garda

Veneto. Meat and dairy products are abundant, with butter, rather than olive oil, used in Lombard cuisine. Cheeses, from the Parmesan-like *grana* to the creamy cows' milk cheeses, appear on every menu, either enriching pastas and risottos or served on a platter with fresh bread and olive oil. Fresh herbs and vegetables, such as *porcini* mushrooms, artichokes, red chicory and asparagus, are key ingredients, grown in abundance and used with fish, meat, risotto and pasta.

Where to Eat

There are dozens of casual, family-run trattorias serving authentic local dishes, as well as more classy and elegant places catering for gourmets. Although traditionally a **ristorante** is smarter, more professional and expensive than a **trattoria**, the difference between the two these days is negligible. An **osteria**, traditionally a tavern or inn serving wine and pasta, can nowadays be any type of restaurant, from traditional to hip. The ubiquitous **pizzeria** usually offers a wide-ranging menu including many types of pasta, meat dishes and even fish, as well as pizzas. The best pizzas come bubbling hot from a wood-fired brick oven (in small towns only available in the evening), the worst are thick-based squares with a thin layer of tomato and cheese topping, served in cafés during the day. *Pizza a taglio*, sold by the slice with a variety of toppings, is the most popular Italian takeaway food item.

An **enoteca** or wine bar will have a wide selection of fine wines with a platter of cheese or cold meats to accompany them. A **tavola calda** is a self-service or takeaway with hot meals such as pasta, risottos, meat and vegetable dishes. For a quick bite go to a **bar** or **café** where you can find a selection of rolls with savoury fillings and *tramezzini* (crustless, generously filled sandwiches). Standing at the bar *(al banco)* is always a lot cheaper than sitting at a table with waiter service.

In the larger resorts a whole string of waterside cafés and pizzerias will be vying for your trade, some advertising a *menu turistico* in several languages. Often the better-value places are in side streets, away from the waterfront or on the edge of town, though it's hard to resist the lakefront views.

What to Eat

As in the rest of Italy, restaurants (as opposed to pizzerias) offer four courses: *antipasto* (the hors d'oeuvre), *primo* (the first course, which is pasta, risotto or soup), *secondo* (the second course, i.e. fish or meat) and finally the *dolce* (dessert). Traditionally you were expected to have at least three courses; nowadays in most establishments it's quite acceptable to opt, say, for an *antipasto* followed by a pasta, or perhaps a pasta followed by a dessert.

Antipasti

The selection of hors d'oeuvres will typically include *antipasto di pesce*, which is likely to be marinated freshwater fish such as *persico* (perch), *tinca* (tench) or *lavarello* (a lake white fish) and an *antipasto di carne*, a selection of cold meats such as thinly sliced *prosciutto crudo* (cured ham), mountain hams, salami, seasoned sausages, smoked beef, *bresaola* (dried salted beef) or, in Trentino, *Speck* (smoked cured ham). The cold cuts will come with bread, extra-virgin olive oil (Lake Garda produces the best) and perhaps with *mostarda de Cremona*, which is

Set menus vary from a basic two- or three-course meal, usually with a choice of meat or fish, to a seven-course blow-out *menu degustazione*, giving you the chance to try several house specialities. All set menus include service and cover charge; some also throw in house wine, mineral water and coffee.

A selection of _antipasti_ in Verona

fruit pickled in a mustard sauce. Around Lake Como, restaurant menus may feature _missoltini_ or _missultitt_, sun-dried salted shad which is lightly grilled and served with oil and vinegar.

Il Primo

Rice is prepared in dozens of different ways, enriched with fish, seafood, meat and vegetables. The ingredients will vary according to the seasons, The most famous rice dish of the region is _risotto alla Milanese_, made with short-grain Arborio rice, stock, beef marrow, onions, saffron and Parmesan cheese. Other popular combinations are _risotto ai funghi_, with mushrooms (often _porcini_ or wild mushrooms); _risotto alla pescatora_ with prawns, squid, mussels and clams; _risotto al nero di seppie_ from the Veneto, coloured and flavoured with the ink of cuttlefish.

Pasta comes in all shapes and sizes, is often home-made and, like risottos, is served with a remarkable range of sauces.

Caoncelli from Bergamo and Brescia is made with spinach, eggs, cheese, amaretti biscuits and breadcrumbs; *strangolapreti* ('priest stranglers') are elongated dumplings made of spinach, bread, eggs and cheese. In addition to regional sauces you are likely to find the popular *al pomodoro*, tomato sauce flavoured with onion, garlic or basil; *alla carbonara*, with eggs, bacon, Parmesan and pecorino cheeses, and *al ragu*, the Neapolitan meat sauce. Soups can be a meal in themselves, especially the delicious *zuppa di pesce*, more of a fish stew than a soup. *Minestrone alla milanese* is vegetable soup with rice and bacon; *zuppa pavese* is a clear broth with egg and bread.

Il Secondo

Try and choose seasonal **fish** from local waters, such as *lavarello*, which may come either stuffed with vegetables and herbs, cooked in a sauce such as garlic and almond or

Fish drying, Sala Comacina

capers and tomatoes, simply served on a spit or perhaps puréed and served with bread. Look out also for *luccio mantecato*, cream of pike, accompanied by polenta; *filetto di pesce persico alle erbe aromatiche*, fillet of perch with aromatic herbs; lake trout *(trota)* stuffed with herbs or perhaps baked with olives, capers and anchovies, or simply

Osso buco, veal shank stew

grilled; and *carpione*, a kind of carp found only in Lake Garda. Most menus also feature fish from the Italian seas (and beyond), such as *branzino* (bass), *orata* (bream), *sogliola* (sole) *gamberoni* (giant prawns), *calamari* (squid) and *vongole* (clams). Non-lake fish may well be frozen – and some of the more upfront restaurants will indicate this with a star against the item. Smaller fish are served whole at a fixed price, the larger species will be charged by the *etto* (100g) and it's wise to check out the price before ordering. Salted dried cod is used in dozens of recipes. From the Veneto, for example, comes *baccalà mantecato*, dried salted cod made into a creamy paste with garlic and olive oil and served with polenta – something of an acquired taste. Also from the Veneto and not to everyone's taste is *sarde in saor*, sardines in a sweet-and-sour sauce.

The main Milanese **meat** specialities are *osso buco*, veal-shank stew; and *costoletta alla milanese*, veal cutlet fried in breadcrumbs (called *wienerschnitzel* in northern Lake Garda). Most menus will feature simply cooked steak, pork, chicken, veal, lamb, duck and often more humble fare such as braised donkey, rabbit casserole, jugged hare or stewed tripe. The

Espresso and *biscotti*

choice will vary according to the season. Around Brescia you may come across *lu-mache alla bresciana*, snails cooked with spinach and served with Parmesan. Polenta often accompanies meat dishes, especially in Trentino and around Bergamo, Brescia and Lake Garda. *Peara* sauce is a Veronese speciality, a blend of breadcrumbs, bone marrow, beef stock, black pepper and Parmesan. The Milanese *cassoeula*, a pork and Savoy cabbage casserole, is served with polenta and traditionally eaten in winter.

Main courses often come with **vegetables** *(contorni)*; salads are ordered and served separately and are almost invariably *verde* (green) or *mista* (mixed). Vegetarian restaurants are a rarity though meat- and fish-free dishes are increasingly available on menus. You might try grilled vegetables as an *antipasto*, then a risotto or pasta with fresh *porcini* or other vegetables.

Desserts don't play a major role on the menus. The usual choice is fruit salad, ice cream, sorbet and perhaps a home-made apple tart or tiramisu (literally 'pick-me-up'), the alcoholic chocolate and coffee gateau from the Veneto. **Cheeses** are abundant, from the soft white ricotta from the mountains; the creamy *robiolo* from the pre-Alpine valleys of Lombardy; the tangy *Taleggio* from Valsassina (Lake Como); to the hard Parmesan-like *grana* from the Padua Plain. Panettone, the large cake containing raisins and candied fruit, is a speciality of Milan; *torrone* is a honey and almond nougat originating from Cremona.

What to Drink

Lombardy produces some excellent red wines, best of which are the dry smooth reds from Valtellina on the Swiss/Italian border near Lake Como. The Oltrepò Pavese zone, in the Po Valley south of Pavia, is Italy's third-largest wine producer, noted for good, full-bodied, dry reds; it also produces Pinot sparkling white wine and a large quantity of Riesling. The hilly Franciacorta region bordering Lake Iseo produces good red and white wine, but is best known for its sparkling *spumante*,

Coffee Break

An Italian café almost invariably serves a decent cup of real coffee. A cappuccino (familiarly called a *cappuccio*), won't be a huge Starbucks-like mug of froth but a normal-sized cup with a generous amount of espresso and a frothy topping. Italians only drink cappuccino for breakfast but are used to foreigners drinking it all day. After around 11am and particularly after meals the locals get their injection of caffeine from a small black espresso. Tourist hotels often have a DIY machine for 'American coffee' at breakfast time, but normally a waiter will be happy to make you an Italian cappuccino at no extra cost. In a region of people-watching piazzas and mesmerizing lake views it's a great temptation to sit for hours over one cup of coffee (or cocktail if you wish), and no one minds if you do. The following is a list of just a few of the different types of coffee served in bars or cafés.

Espresso or *caffè* – small and black

Caffè lungo – weaker coffee

Caffe doppio – double espresso

Caffè latte – milky coffee

Caffè macchiato – small espresso with a dash of milk

Caffè corretto – with grappa, brandy or other liqueur

Caffè freddo – iced coffee

Decaffeinato or *decaff* – decaffeinated coffee

Valpolicella from Verona

which makes an excellent aperitif. Lake Garda's best wines are still white and sparkling Bianco di Custoza, and dry red Bardolino, which you can try at the Museo del Vino in Bardolino (<www.zeni.it>) and buy very cheaply in and around the town. The Verona region produces the famous white Soave, red Valpolicella and the lesser-known but top-quality smooth red Recioto, best served with dessert.

House wine, *vino della casa*, is variable but usually very acceptable and always reasonably priced. In the cheaper eateries it is served in litre or half-litre carafes or jugs. The more sophisticated establishments will produce a hefty wine list featuring international as well as local and Italian wines. In wine-growing regions such as Bardolino, it's always worth opting for the very reasonably priced local wines.

A good meal is usually concluded with a *digestivo*, such as a brandy, *grappa* (the variable local firewater made from grape skins) or *limoncello*, made from lemons.

To Help You Order...

A table for one/two/three.	**Un tavolo per una persona/ per due/per tre.**
I would like…	**Vorrei…**
The bill, please.	**Il conto, per favore.**

...and Read the Menu

aglio	garlic	lumache	snails
agnello	lamb	maiale	pork
aragosta	lobster	manzo	beef
asino	donkey	melanzane	aubergine
baccalà	salted cod		(eggplant)
basilico	basil	olio	oil
birra	beer	olive	olives
bistecca	beefsteak	orata	bream
branzino	bass	pane	bread
bresaola	cured beef	panna	cream
burro	butter	patate	potatoes
calamari	squid	peperoni	peppers
capretto	kid	persico	perch
carciofi	artichokes	pesce	fish
cavallo	horse	piselli	peas
cinghiale	wild boar	pollo	chicken
cipolle	onions	polpo/pólipo	octopus
coniglio	rabbit	pomodori	tomatoes
cozze	mussels	prosciutto	ham
fagioli	beans	riso	rice
fagiolini	green beans	salsiccie	sausages
finocchio	fennel	sogliola	sole
formaggio	cheese	spinaci	spinach
frittata	omelette	tinca	tench
fritto misto	mixed fried	tonno	tuna
	fish	trota	trout
frutti di mare	seafood	uova	eggs
funghi	mushrooms	verdure	vegetables
gamberetti	shrimps	vitello	veal
gamberi	prawns	vino	wine
gamberoni	giant prawns	vongole	clams
gelato	ice cream	zucchini	courgettes
insalata	salad	zuppa	soup

HANDY TRAVEL TIPS

An A–Z Summary of Practical Information

A

ACCOMMODATION

Accommodation in the region is plentiful and ranges from grandiose lakeside villas to simple bed and breakfasts and farmhouses. Prices, which have to be displayed in guest rooms, vary according to t he season, being at their highest in midsummer. Many of the hotels on the lakes close in winter.

The busiest times are Easter, July and August, or any weekend from Easter to autumn. For these periods it is advisable to book well ahead. Hotels normally require confirmation of a reservation, which can be done (in English) by email or fax. In high season some hotels require you to stay for a minimum of three nights, and those with restaurants may only offer half- or full-board rates. A deposit of at least one night's stay, payable by credit card, is usually requested. Failure to turn up or to inform the hotel in advance of cancellation will normally incur the loss of a night's deposit.

If you arrive on spec, local tourist offices will advise on available accommodation and may do the booking for you. If possible, check out the guest room before committing to a reservation. Rooms can vary hugely, both in size and outlook. Prices normally reflect the difference, and it's usually worth stretching the budget to secure the more desirable rooms. In lakeside resorts, hotels are often located across the main road from the lake, with noisy rooms at the front. Single rooms, unless you are in a luxury hotel, are usually small and viewless; but for a bit extra you can often opt for a '*doppia uso singola*', a double for single use, or a small double room.

Breakfast is normally included in the overnight room rate. Depending on the category of hotel this will vary from a dull crusty roll with packaged butter and jam to a great spread of cereals, cheeses, cold cuts, yoghurts, croissants, home-made pastries and fresh fruit. If breakfast is not included in the room rate it is usually better value to pop out for a cappuccino and croissant in the local café.

An appealing alternative to hotel accommodation is *agriturismi*, working farms and other rural properties which rent out rooms or self-contained apartments to tourists. These have sprouted around the lakes region, many in peaceful locations well away from the lakeside resorts. Some offer breakfast and an evening meal, which is based on home-grown produce. Meals are communal affairs, often around the kitchen table. However, not all *agriturismi* conform to the picturesque farmhouse image – many are modern properties in unremarkable settings. Details of *agriturismi* are supplied by local tourist offices – or visit <www.agriturist.com>.

Bed and breakfasts in private homes are growing in number, both around the lakes and in the towns. Tourist offices can supply you with details, or visit <www.bbitalia.net>.

AIRPORTS

The lakes region has no less than five airports, including the three that serve Milan. For the lakes in the west of the region (Orta, Maggiore and Como), the most convenient arrival points are Milan's Malpensa airport, 50km (31 miles) northwest of Milan (<www.aeroportimilano.it>) or Orio al Serio airport at Bergamo, 48km (30 miles) northeast of Milan (<www.sacbo.it>). This is also the ideal arrival point if you are heading to Lake Iseo. For Milan, Linate airport (<www.aeroportimilano.it>), 10km (6 miles) to the east, is by far the closest airport to the city.

For Lake Garda's western shore, the quickest gateway is Brescia's airport (<www.aeroportobrescia.it>), 20km (12½ miles) southeast of Brescia, which confusingly has three different names: 'Gabriele d'Annunzio', 'Brescia-Montichiari' and 'Verona (Brescia)'. If you are hiring a car the airport is also worth considering for access to Verona (52km/32 miles), Cremona (47km/29 miles) and Bergamo (65km/40 miles). Another useful gateway for Lake Garda, particularly the eastern shore, is Valerio Catullo Airport, also called Verona-Villafranca (<www.aeroportoverona.it>), which is only 15km (9.5 miles) from Verona. For the east shores of Lake Garda you could also consider the Venice airports of Marco Polo and Treviso which are less than an hour away.

Bergamo's Orio al Serio airport, used by Ryanair and other low-cost airlines, is linked by a half-hourly shuttle bus service to both Bergamo, 5km (3 miles) away, and to Milan's Stazione Centrale (Central Station). The airport has two banks with 24-hour Bancomat service, foreign exchange bureaux, a left-luggage office and a very helpful, well-stocked tourist office for visitors to Bergamo and the surrounding area. Milan's Malpensa and Linate airports are both equipped with banks, currency exchange, internet access and left-luggage facilities. The small Gabriele d'Annunzio airport is linked to Brescia and Verona by regular shuttle buses; and from Valerio Catullo airport there are buses to the railway station of Verona every 20 minutes from 6.30am to 11.30pm.

| What time does the train/bus leave for the city centre? | **A che ora parte il treno/pullman per in centro?** |

BICYCLE HIRE

Bikes can be hired in all the towns and resorts, but prices are quite steep. Local tourist offices can supply details of local bike-hire outlets as well as trail guides in popular biking regions. Hills and mountains have signposted tracks of varying degrees of difficulty. A few hotels lend their guests bikes free of charge.

B

BUDGETING FOR YOUR TRIP

In high season you can expect to pay around €120–170 for a comfortable double room with bath, €50–95 in a simple hotel. A good three-course meal without wine in a restaurant will cost from

€30–50, a light lunch €10–20. In general the best-value accommodation and restaurants are located away from the lakefronts. Coffee and soft drinks are €1.50–3.50, beer €2–4, aperitif or cocktail with canapés €3–8. It is worth bearing in mind that, as in the rest of Italy, coffee or drinks taken at the bar are far cheaper than those taken at a table with waiter service. Entry fees to museums, archaeological sites and gardens vary from €1–8; entrance is free for EU citizens under 18 and over 65. Opera tickets in Verona cost from €12–145.

C

CAMPING

Campsites are dotted around all the main lakes and range from basic sites to four-star affairs with swimming pools, restaurants and other facilities. Lake Garda has far the widest choice, with sites all round the shores and a profusion in the south. Details are available in the tourist accommodation booklets from regional tourist offices or on the internet at <www.camping.it> where you can book online. Campsites are normally open from April to September and are at their most crowded from mid-July to late August.

Is there a campsite near here? **C'e un campeggio qui vicino?**

CAR HIRE

Hiring a car is essential if you're planning a touring holiday, though the traffic and tunnels along many of the lakeside roads don't lead to leisurely driving. Car-hire bookings made in advance on the internet work out cheaper than hiring on arrival. In high season a small car will cost from around €250 a week, including third-party liability and taxes, but excluding insurance excess. Make sure you check all extras when comparing quotes from different companies. The major car-hire companies have offices in the main cities and airports. Drivers must present their own national driving licence or one that is internationally recognised. There is a small additional charge for an extra driver. Credit-card imprints are taken as a deposit and are normally the only form of payment acceptable. 'Inclusive' prices do not normally include personal accident insurance or insurance against damage to windscreens, tyres and wheels.

I would like to hire a car	**Vorrei noleggiare una macchina**
for one day	**per un giorno**
for one week	**per una settimana**
I want full insurance.	**Voglio l'assicurazione completa.**

CLIMATE

The holiday season for the lakes is Easter to October. The best time to go is spring, early summer or autumn, ideal times being May, June and September when it's warm and sunny but not as crowded, hot or muggy as midsummer. In July and August temperatures can soar to 30°C, though the lakes, with a gentle breeze, are slightly cooler than the cities. The wettest months are October and November. Winters are foggy and cold with chilly winds from the Alps. Most places around the lakes close down for the season and ferry services are limited.

	J	F	M	A	M	J	J	A	S	O	N	D
°C	5	8	13	18	23	27	29	29	24	17	10	6
°F	40	46	56	65	74	80	84	85	75	63	51	43

CRIME AND SAFETY

It is wise to take simple precautions against pickpockets. Avoid carrying large amounts of cash around with you and leave important documents and valuables in the hotel safe. Keep a firm hold of handbags, especially when using public transport or shopping at markets. For insurance purposes, theft and loss must be reported straightaway to the police. In case of theft take photocopies of flight tickets, driving licence, passport and insurance documents.

I want to report a theft.	**Vorrei denunciare un furto.**
My wallet/passport/ticket has been stolen	**Mi hanno rubato il portafoglio/ il passaporto/il biglietto**

CUSTOMS AND ENTRY REQUIREMENTS

For citizens of EU countries a valid passport or identity card is all that is needed to enter Italy for stays of up to 90 days. Citizens of the US, Canada, Australia and New Zealand require only a valid passport.

Visas *(permesso di soggiorno)*. For stays of more than 90 days a visa is required. Contact your country's Italian Embassy.

Customs. Free exchange of non duty-free goods for personal use is allowed between EU countries. Those from non-EU countries should refer to their home country's regulating organisation for a current complete list of import restrictions.

Currency restrictions. Tourists may bring an unlimited amount of Italian or foreign currency into the country. On departure you must declare any currency beyond the equivalent of €12,500, so it's wise to declare sums exceeding this amount when you arrive.

D

DRIVING

If taking your own car from the UK you should allow for tolls on French, Swiss, German and Italian motorways. To take your car into Italy, you will need an international driving licence or valid national one, car registration documents, a red warning triangle in case of breakdown, a national identity sticker for your car, and headlamp deflectors. A green insurance card (an extension to your ordinary insurance) is not compulsory but advisable in case of an accident.

Tolls are levied on the motorway but it's worth the relatively small expense to cover ground fast. Signposting on main and rural roads is quite good, but beware of reckless drivers and motorcyclists.

Are we on the right road for…? **Siamo sulla strada giusta per…?**

Rules of the road. Drive on the right, pass on the left. Speed limits in Italy are 50km/h (30mph) in towns and built-up areas, 90km/h (55mph) on main roads and 130km/h (80mph) on motorways. At roundabouts the traffic from the right has the right of way. Seat belts are compulsory in the front and back, and children should be properly restrained. The use of hand-held mobile telephones while driving is prohibited. The blood alcohol limit is 0.08 percent and police occasionally make random breath tests.

Breakdowns. In case of accident or breakdown call 113 (General Emergencies) or the Automobile Club of Italy on 116. The club has an efficient 24-hour service which is available to foreign visitors.

Petrol. Petrol is readily available, though many service stations close for three hours over the lunch period. On main roads there are plenty of 24-hour stations with self-service dispensers accepting euro notes and major credit cards. The majority but certainly not all stations accept credit cards.

Parking. Parking is not expensive but it can be difficult finding spaces in the centre of towns and lakeside resorts at busy times of the year. Parking in towns is controlled by meters or scratch cards, available from tobacconists and bars. The larger towns have multi-storey car parks. Some free parking is controlled by parking discs (if you have hired a car a disc will be provided). Parking in Milan is notoriously difficult and to be discouraged

I've had a breakdown	**Ho avuto un guasto**
There's been an accident	**C'è stato un incidente**
Fill it up please	**Faccia il pieno per favore**
Super/normal/	**super/normale**
Lead-free/diesel	**senza piombo/gasolio**
Where's the nearest car park?	**Dov'è il parcheggio più vicino?**
Can I park here?	**Posso parcheggiare qui?**

E

ELECTRICITY

220V/50Hz AC is standard. Sockets take two-pin, round-pronged plugs. UK appliances will require an adaptor, American 11V appliances a transformer.

EMBASSIES AND CONSULATES

If you lose your passport or need other help, contact your nearest national embassy or consulate.

Australia: Via Borgogna 2, Milan, tel: 02 77704227, <www.italy.embassy.gov.au>.

Canada: Canadian Consulate General, Via Vittor Pisani, 19, Milan, tel: 02 67581, <www.canada.it>.

Ireland: Piazza S. Pietro in Gessate 2, Milan, tel: 02 55187569.

New Zealand: Via Guido D'Arezzo 6, Milan, tel: 02 4990201, email: <nzemb.rom@flashnet.it>.

UK: British Consulate, Via San Paolo 7, Milan, tel: 02 723001, <www.britain.it>.

US: US Embassy, Via Principe Amedeo 2/10, Milan, tel: 02 290351, <www.usembassy.it>.

EMERGENCIES

Police	**112**
General Emergency	**113**
Fire	**115**
Ambulance	**118**

G

GAY AND LESBIAN TRAVELLERS

Milan, along with Bologna, is the most gay-friendly city in Italy. The lakes region, however, is more conservative and, although not necessarily averse to gay couples travelling together, the locals do not always tolerate overt displays of affection. Larger towns like Brescia have gay bars and discos; for information contact Arci-Gay, Via Bezzecca 3, Milan, tel: 02 54122225, <www.arcigay.it>. Bergamo has a handful of gay venues, including the Club Haus Bar, Via delle Canovine 26/a, tel: 035 4592123 and the City Sauna Club, Via delle Clementina 8, tel: 035 240418. Verona has a couple of places outside the centre: the City Sauna Club, Via Giolfino 12, tel: 338 4037781 and beside it Romeo's Club, a disco bar, tel: 338 4037781.

GETTING THERE

By air. Ryanair, tel: 0871 246 0000, <www.ryanair.com>, flies from five UK airports to 'Milan-Bergamo' (Bergamo's Orio al Serio airport); and also from Stansted to Verona (Brescia). **EasyJet**, tel: 0905 821 0905, <www.easyjet.com>, flies from Gatwick to Milan's Linate and Malpensa airports. **British Airways**, tel: 0870 850 9850, <www.ba.com> and **Alitalia**, tel: 0870 5448259, <www.alitalia.it> have regular flights from Heathrow to both Linate and Malpensa; BA also flies from Birmingham and Manchester to Malpensa, and from Gatwick to Verona-Villafranca.

By car. The quickest route to Milan from the UK channel ports takes a minimum of 12 hours, over a distance of 1,040km (650 miles). For route planning and details on the cost of petrol, road tolls (levied on French and Italian motorways) and the Swiss motorway road tax, visit <www.viamichelin.com>.

By rail. Travelling by train to Italy normally works out more expensive than taking a flight with a low-cost airline. The journey from the UK to Milan via Paris on Eurostar (<www.eurostar.com>) and then via Switzerland takes 15 hours. From Milan there are fast train services to all the main lakes. For information in the UK on tickets, rail passes and to book online, contact Rail Choice, <www.railchoice.co.uk>, for rail travel within Italy visit <www.tren italia.com>.

GUIDES AND TOURS

Local tourist offices, travel agencies and hotels can provide details of guides and tours. There is no shortage of choice whether it's a guided city tour, a cruise or dinner dance on a ferry, a Romeo and Juliet tour in Verona or an excursion to the cellars and vineyards in the wine-producing regions.

H

HEALTH AND MEDICAL CARE

All EU countries have reciprocal arrangements for reclaiming the costs of medical services, and residents should obtain the European Health Insurance Card (available in the UK from post offices or online <www.ehic.org.uk>). This only covers you for medical care, not for emergency repatriation costs or additional expenses such as accommodation and flights for anyone travelling with you. To cover all eventualities a travel insurance policy is advisable, and

I need a doctor/dentist	**Ho bisogno di un medico/dentista**
Where is the nearest chemist?	**Dov'è la farmacia più vicina?**

for non-EU residents, essential. For insurance claims keep all receipts for medical treatment and any medicines prescribed. Vaccinations are not needed for Italy, but take with you sunscreen and mosquito repellent in the summer. Tap water is safe to drink unless you see the sign *acqua non potabile*. However, many visitors prefer to do as the locals and drink mineral water.

A pharmacy *(farmacia)* is identified by a green cross. All main towns offer a 24-hour pharmacy service, with a night-time and Sunday rota. After-hour locations are listed in local papers and posted on all pharmacy doors. Italian pharmacists are well-trained to deal with minor ailments and although they do not stock quantities of foreign medicines they can usually supply the local equivalent. If you need a doctor *(medico)* ask at the pharmacy or at your hotel. For serious cases or emergencies, dial 118 for an ambulance or head for the *Pronto Soccorso* (Accident and Emergency) of the local hospital. This will also deal with emergency dental treatment.

L

LANGUAGE

Staff in hotels and shops in the main resorts speak English, but a smattering of Italian will come in useful if you're off-the-beaten-track. On the Swiss side of the lakes less English is spoken than German.

M

MAPS

Touring Club Italiano (TCI) produces detailed, easy-to-read maps of the region which are widely available. Their 1:175,000 Lakes of Lombardy map is useful for the main lakes, except Garda which is covered in the TCI 1:175,000 map to Lake Garda (including Verona). TCI also publish the 1:200,000 map to Lombardy. Local tourist offices can normally provide you with free town and area maps.

MEDIA

Newspapers. English-language newspapers can be found in main towns and resorts, usually on the day of publication

Television and Radio. Many hotels provide satellite TV, which broadcasts 24-hour English-language news channels. The Italian state TV network, RAI (Radio Televisione Italiana), broadcasts three TV channels, RAI 1, 2 and 3, and there are half a dozen private channels pouring out soaps, films, quiz shows and nonstop ads. The state-run radio stations, RAI 1, 2 and 3, mainly broadcast news, chat and music.

MONEY

Currency. Since January 2002 the unit of currency in Italy has been the euro (€) divided into 100 cents. Euro notes come in denominations of 500, 200, 100, 50, 20, 10 and 5; coins come in denominations of 2 and 1 euros, then 50, 20, 10, 5, 2 and 1 cents. In Switzerland the currency is the Swiss franc. In Swiss resorts you can usually pay with euros but your change will be in Swiss francs, and normally at a poor exchange rate.

Exchange Facilities. Banks and post offices tend to offer the best rates, followed by exchange offices and hotels. Some bureaux de change offer commission-free facilities, but check first that the rate of exchange is not higher than that of the banks.

Credit Cards and ATMs. The major international credit cards are accepted in the majority of hotels and restaurants, stores and super-

I want to change some pounds/dollars	**Desidero cambiare delle sterline/dei dollari**
Do you accept traveller's cheques?	**Accetta travellers cheques?**
Can I pay with a credit card?	**Posso pagare con la carta di credito?**
Where is the bank?	**Dov'è la banca?**

markets, but some simple hotels, B&Bs and trattorias only accept cash. ATMs (Bancomats) are widespread, but banks take a hefty commission – it is usually better value to use cash only when essential and pay off larger amounts such as restaurant bills and pricier items in shops by credit card.

Traveller's Cheques. If security is a priority, these are the best bet. They can only be used by the purchaser and if lost or stolen they will be refunded. The cheques can be exchanged on presentation of a passport at banks, exchange offices, hotels and some shops. The cheques tend to attract a high percentage of commission and sometimes a transaction fee on top. Traveller's cheques are widely accepted.

OPENING HOURS

Banks generally open Mon–Fri 8am–1.30pm and 3–4pm (afternoon opening times may vary). Banks at airports and main stations usually have longer opening hours and are open at weekends.

Museums have varying opening hours; the main ones open all day every day, but some small museums close for 2–3 hours over the lunch period and all day on Monday.

Villas/Gardens usually open all day every day in season.

Churches normally close at lunch time (noon–3pm or later). Sightseeing on Sunday morning, when services take place, is discouraged.

Shops are normally open from Mon–Sat 9am–1pm, 3.30/4–7.30/8pm. In main cities many shops open all day, and on Sundays too.

P

POLICE

The city police or *polizia urbana* regulate traffic and enforce laws, while the *carabinieri* are the armed military police who handle law and order. The *polizia stradale* patrol the highways and other roads.

In an emergency the *carabinieri* can be reached on 112 – or you can ring the general emergency number, 113.

Where's the nearest police station?	**Dov'è il posto di polizia più vicino?**

POST OFFICES

Post offices normally open Mon–Fri 8.15am–2pm, Sat 8.15am–noon or 2pm. Stamps *(francobolli)* can also be bought from tobacconists.

Where's the nearest post office?	**Dov'è l'ufficio postale più vicino?**
I'd like a stamp for this letter/postcard	**Desidero un francobollo per questa lettera/cartolina**

PUBLIC HOLIDAYS

Shops, banks, museums and galleries usually close on the days listed below. When a national holiday falls on a Friday or a Monday, Italians may make a *ponte* (bridge) or long weekend.

January 1	*Capodanno*	New Year's Day
January 6	*Epifania*	Epiphany
March/April	*Pasqua*	Easter
March/April	*Lunedì di Pasqua*	Easter Monday
25 April	*Festa della Liberazione*	Liberation Day
1 May	*Festa del Lavoro*	Labour Day
15 August	*Ferragosto*	Assumption Day
1 November	*Ognissanti*	All Saints' Day
8 December	*L'Immacolata Concezione*	Feast of the Immaculate Conception
25 December	*Natale*	Christmas Day
26 December	*Santo Stefano*	St Stephen's Day

PUBLIC TRANSPORT

By bus. Regular, reasonably priced buses link towns and villages along lakeshores. Tickets cannot be purchased on board, but are available from tobacconists and newsstands or at bus stations and must be stamped when you board the bus.

By boat. Ferries, hydrofoils and excursion cruisers operate services on all the main lakes. Hydrofoils *(aliscafi)* are faster than ferries *(battelli)* but are more expensive and have inside seating only. Useful car ferries *(traghetti)* link Intra and Laveno on Lake Maggiore; Menaggio, Varenna, Cadenabbia and Bellagio on Lake Como; and Maderno to Torri del Benaco and Limone to Malcesine on Lake Garda.

Timetables are available from ticket offices, tourist information offices and other outlets, or online at <www.navlaghi.it> (lakes Maggiore, Como and Garda) or <www.navigazionelagoiseo.it> (Lake Iseo). Tickets can normally be bought at the point of departure; if bought on board they are a bit more expensive. Ferries normally run from 7am to about 7pm, though in summer the main lakes also offer an evening ferry trip with dinner and dancing on board.

By rail. For main-line train information visit Trenitalia on <www.trenitalia.com>. Milan is a major rail junction with excellent, reasonably priced services to the main lakes and towns across the region. The lakes themselves, however, are better served by ferries and buses. The cost of rail travel is cheap in comparison to other European countries. The price of a journey depends on the type of train. You can either take the slower services which stop at all the towns or the fast Intercity, Eurocity or Eurostar trains which levy a supplement of at least 30 percent and require seat reservations. It is advisable to make a reservation well in advance. Italian ticket offices have notoriously long queues – though some of the bigger stations now have automatic machines to issue tickets (with instructions in English). Return tickets offer no saving on two singles. Tickets must be stamped in the yellow machines at the near end of the platforms before boarding the train. Tickets bought on the train incur a very hefty supplement.

When's the next bus/train to …?	**Quando parte il prossimo autobus/treno per….?**
Where can I buy a ticket?	**Dov'è posso comprare un biglietto?**
single (one-way)	**andata**
return	**andata e ritorno**

Taxis. Taxis can be found in main squares in the larger towns. Beware of touts without meters – especially near airports and train stations. Taxi fares are quite high and there are additional charges, posted in the taxis, for luggage, trips at night and on Sundays and holidays.

R

RELIGION

Like the rest of Italy the region is primarily Roman Catholic. The church still plays a major role in the community though numbers of regular worshippers have been in decline for some years. Local patron saints' days are celebrated, such as San Giovanni Battista on Lake Como *(see page 95)*, but religious festivals are not as commonplace as in southern Italy. Milan has congregations of all the main religions (for details consult <www.hellomilano.it> under the 'Worship' section in Useful Information).

S

SMOKING

In January 2005, Italy became the third country in Europe (after Ireland and Norway) to ban smoking in indoor public places. This includes bars and restaurants unless they have a separate area for smokers (very few do). Fines of up to €2,000 can be imposed on restaurant and bar owners who do not enforce the ban.

T

TELEPHONES

Telecom Italia public telephones are widespread and have instructions in English. Calls are made with a pre-paid phone card (*scheda* or *carta telefonica*) available in denominations of €5, €10 and €20 and available from Telecom offices, tobacconists or newsstands. Pre-paid international telephone cards (from €5), available at post offices, travel agents and other outlets are far better value if you are phoning abroad. With these you call a free phone number, dial the PIN code on your card and then the number (clear instructions are given in English). Calls can also be made with a charge card bought from your telephone company prior to travel. This is useful for telephoning from hotels which levy hefty surcharges on long-distance calls.

When phoning abroad, dial the international code, followed by the city or area code and then the number. Off-peak rate for international calls in Italy is Mon–Sat 10pm–8am, Sun 1pm–Mon 8am. For an English-speaking operator and international reverse charge calls dial 170 and for international directory enquiries dial 176. Numbers beginning 800 are free. Italian area codes have all been incorporated into the numbers, so even if you are calling from the same town that you are telephoning, the code must be included.

Mobile phones (cellphones). In order to function within Italy some mobiles need to be activated with a roaming facility or need to be 'unblocked' for use abroad. Check with your mobile company before leaving. Charges for using a UK-based mobile to make and receive calls and texts abroad are notoriously high and it is worth checking with your phone company how much you will be paying and which local network gives the best value. You can then set it to the cheapest network on arrival. You can also bar incoming calls, or on some mobiles limit them to specified numbers. If you are in Italy for some time it's worth purchasing an Italian SIM 'pay as you go' (*scheda prepagata*) with a new mobile number for the length of your stay. To do

so you will need your passport or ID card. The SIM card can be bought from any mobile shop in Italy; or you can purchase a card before you go via <www.uk2abroad.com> and keep your mobile number.
Country codes. Australia +61; Ireland +353; New Zealand +64; South Africa +27, UK +44; US and Canada +1.

TIME ZONES

Italy is one hour ahead of Greenwich Mean Time (GMT). From the last Sunday in March to the last Sunday in October, clocks are put forward one hour. The following box shows times across the globe when it is midday in Milan.

New York	London	**Milan**	Jo'burg	Sydney
6am	11am	**noon**	1pm	8pm

TIPPING

In restaurants a *coperto* or cover charge of €1.50–4 is usually charged for service and bread. Tipping is not customary in Italy, though a bit extra will be appreciated. For quick service in bars, leave a coin or two with your till receipt when ordering. Taxi drivers do not expect a tip but will appreciate it if you round up the fare to the next euro.

Thank you, this is for you.	**Grazie, questo è per lei.**
Keep the change.	**Tenga il resto.**

TOILETS

Public toilets are rare. If you use the facilities of cafés and bars, it will be appreciated if you buy a drink.

Where are the toilets please?	**Dove sono i gabinetti, per favore?**

TOURIST INFORMATION

Italian Tourist Offices Abroad

Canada: Suite 907, South Tower, 175 Bloor Street East, Toronto, Ontario M4W3R8, tel: 416-925 4882, <www.italiantourism.com>.

UK: 1 Princes Street, London W1B 2AY, tel: 020 7408 1254; <www.enit.it>.

US: <www.italiantourism.com>; 630 Fifth Avenue, Suite 1565, New York, NY 10111, tel: 212-245 5618; 500 North Michigan Avenue, Suite 2240, Chicago, Illinois 60611, tel: 312-644 0996; 12400 Wilshire Boulevard, Suite 550, Los Angeles, CA 90025, tel: 310-820 1898.

Regional Tourist Offices

Stresa: Piazza Marconi 16, tel: 0323 31308/30150, <www.stresa.org>.

Como: Piazza Cavour 17, tel: 031 269712, <www.provincia.como.it/turismo>.

Sirmione: Viale Marconi 2, tel: 030 916114, <www.sirmione.it>.

Bergamo: Viale Vittorio Emanuele 20, Città Bassa, tel: 035 210204; Vicolo Aquila Nera 2, Città Alta, tel: 035 232730; there is also a very helpful tourist office at Bergamo's Orio al Serio airport, <www.provincia.bergamo.it>.

Verona: Via degli Alpini 9 (Piazza Brà), tel: 045 8068680; there are also branches at the station and airport, <www.tourism.verona.it>.

Milan: The APT (Azienda di Promozione Turistica) and the IAT (Ufficio Informazione e di Accoglienza Turistica) are both at Via Marconi 1, on the corner of Piazza del Duomo and Via Marconi. (tel: 02 72524301, <www.milanoinfotourist.it>)

Where is the tourist office?   **Dov'è l'ufficio turistico?**

W

WEBSITES AND INTERNET

The official Italian Government Tourist Board site is <www.enit.
it> which has links for the different regions covered by the lakes.

The following are official tourist board sites for the lakes:

<www.distrettolaghi.it> Lake Orta and the west of Lake Maggiore.

<www.turismo.provincia.varese.it> the province of Varese including Lake Maggiore's east side.

<www.lakecomo.com> Lake Como.

<www.gardatrentinonline.it> Lake Garda, Trentino.

<www.tourism.verona.it> Verona province including the east side
of Lake Garda – in Italian only.

For websites of tourist offices in the main towns see TOURIST
INFORMATION.

You can use the internet facilities in most hotels though there is
often a charge for doing so. Towns and main resorts have internet
points, either in cybercafés, which are open all day and evening, or
in offices which usually close for at least two hours in the afternoon.
Tourist offices can supply you with a list of local internet points.

Y

YOUTH HOSTELS

The lakes region only has a dozen or so youth hostels. Verona has a
splendidly located youth hostel in the 16th-century Villa Frances-
catti looking down on the city. (Salita Fontana del Ferro 15, tel: 045
590360). It is open all year round. Milan has several, the main one
being the Ostello Piero Rotta, northwest of the centre at Viale
Salmoiraghi, tel: 02 39267095. An HI (Hostelling International)
card is normally required for youth hostels but temporary member-
ship is available on-the-spot. For information and reservations log
on to <www.ostellionline.org>.

Recommended Hotels

All hotels are officially categorised from one to five stars, or, at the very top end of the scale, 5-star deluxe. The stars assigned denote facilities (such as air conditioning, pool or health club) and are no real indicator of charm or atmosphere. At the top end of the market are the exclusive villa hotels on Lake Como, which fetch some of the highest prices in Italy.

In high season, hotels with their own restaurant may insist on half board, with stays of no less than three days. Lakeside hotels usually charge a supplement for lake views and it is usually worth paying the extra. Many of the hotels in the lakes close for winter, but those in the cities stay open all year. Booking ahead is recommended in high season.

The symbols below are a rough indication of what you can expect to pay in high season for a twin room with bathroom, including breakfast, taxes and service.

€€€€	over 350 euros
€€€	200–350 euros
€€	130–200 euros
€	below 130 euros

LAKE MAGGIORE

BORROMEO ISLANDS

Hotel Ristorante Verbano €€ *Isola dei Pescatori, tel: 0323 30408, fax: 0323 33129, <www.hotelverbano.it>.* A delightful alternative to the grand old hotels of Stresa, the Verbano is a 5-minute ferry ride away on the tiny Isola dei Pescatori. The simple pink villa and its restaurant terraces enjoy romantic views of the lake and Isola Bella. The 12 guest rooms, all named after flowers, have parquet floors, handsome antiques and large bathrooms. The island is busy with tourists by day, but delightfully peaceful at night. The hotel provides a private boat service to Stresa at night when the ferry service ends.

CANNERO RIVIERA

Cannero €–€€ *Piazza Umberto 12, tel: 0323 788046, fax: 0323 788048, <www.hotelcannero.com>.* In a fine lake setting, this is a traditional hotel in what was formerly a monastery and an adjacent private mansion. Family-run and friendly, it provides first-class service and delightful guest rooms. Facilities include a sitting room with foreign-language books, an open-air pool, tennis court and restaurant with lakeside terrace.

CANNOBIO

Cannobio €€ *Piazza Vittorio Emanuele III 6, tel: 0323 739639, fax: 0323 739596, <www.hotelcannobio.com>.* A long-established hotel with a delightful setting on the lakefront by the old harbour. The décor successfully combines the original features of the historic building with contemporary colours and designs.

Pironi €€ *Via Marconi 35, tel: 0323 70624, fax: 0323 72184, <www.pironihotel.it>.* Twelve comfortable rooms in a beautifully converted medieval Franciscan monastery in the picturesque centre of Cannobio. The three-star hotel is furnished with antiques and retains wonderful original features such as frescoes, vaulted ceilings and old stone columns, but unfortunately does not have lake views.

LUINO

Camin Hotel Colmegna €€ *Via A.Palazzi 1, Colmegna (3km/2 miles north of Luino), tel: 0332 510855, fax: 0332 501687, <www.camin-hotels.com>.* The villa was built on the lake in the early 18th century as part of a hunting estate and retains a large park with romantic trails and a waterfall. Facilities include a private beach, a small stone harbour where motorboats can be rented and lake-side terraces for summer meals.

STRESA

Grand Hotel des Iles Borromées €€€€ *Corso Umberto I 67, tel: 0323 938938, fax: 0323 32405, <www.borromees.it>*. The grandest hotel on Lake Maggiore, where literary luminaries such as Ernest Hemingway, George Bernard Shaw and John Steinbeck, as well as numerous European royals, have stayed (you can stay in Hemingway's room for €3,000 a night). Sumptuous public rooms are decorated with Murano chandeliers, stucco and antiques; many of the luxurious guest rooms have fabulous views of the Borromeo islands and the Alps. Facilities include one indoor and two outdoor swimming pools, tennis court, private heliport and landing for boats.

LAKE COMO

ARGEGNO

Villa Belvedere €€–€€€ *Via Milano 8, tel: 031 821116, fax: 031 821571, <www.villabelvedere-argegno.it>*. An alluring villa hotel right on the lake, with glorious views from the terrace where meals are served in summer. The villa has 18 simply furnished rooms – it's worth paying extra for the ones with lake views. Argegno is a small village with a landing stage close to the hotel for ferry trips of Lake Como.

BELLAGIO

Bellagio €–€€ *Salita Grandi 6, tel: 031 950424, fax: 031 951966, <www.hotelbellagio.it>*. Immaculate new boutique hotel set up a flight of steps from the lakeside. There are 29 fresh, spotless rooms with white walls and wood floors, around half of which have lake views. Guests receive a 10-percent discount when dining at the restaurant of the better-known sister Hotel du Lac on the waterfront.

Florence €€ *Piazza Mazzini 46, tel: 031 950342, fax: 031 951722, <www.hotelflorencebellagio.it>*. An 18th-century villa (with a later extension) which has been in the same family for over 100 years. The beamed and vaulted foyer combines traditional furnishings with modern colours and innovative works of art. The shady lakeside terrace is an idyllic spot for a drink or summer dining. Comfortable bedrooms in classical style are priced according to views – most look out on to the lake. The spa offers massage, aromatherapy, sauna and jacuzzi.

Grand Hotel Villa Serbelloni €€€€ *Via Roma 1, tel: 031 950216, fax: 031 951529, <www.villaserbelloni.com>.* Built as a luxury villa on the banks of the lake for an aristocratic family from Milan, this was converted to a hotel in 1873. Royalty, famous politicians and film stars have stayed here. Grand and opulent public rooms boast crystal chandeliers, stuccowork, marble, gilding and antiques. Guest rooms are somewhat old fashioned but are fitted, of course, with 21st-century facilities and are a good deal cheaper than those of Villa d'Este *(see below)*.

CADENABBIA DI GRIANTE

Alberghetto della Marianna € *Via Regina 57, tel and fax: 0344 43095, <www.la-marianna.com>.* A home-from-home bed and breakfast with eight simply-furnished rooms overlooking the lake. Small and friendly, it is run by Paola, who is very hospitable and will help you arrange the day's itinerary. Guests receive a 15-percent discount at La Cucina della Marianna restaurant on the same premises and part-run by Paola's husband.

CERNOBBIO

Villa d'Este €€€€ *Via Regina 40, tel: 031 3481, fax: 031 348873, <www.villadeste.it>.* A famous and palatial 16th-century villa in luxuriant gardens on the outskirts of Cernobbio. Guest rooms are individually furnished with period furniture and Como silk fabrics. The roll call of famous guests includes J.F. Kennedy, Alfred Hitchcock and Madonna. Facilities include a choice of restaurants, a disco at weekends, watersports, a golf course, eight tennis courts, a squash court, a gym, a beauty centre, an indoor and a lake-floating swimming pool, and a helipad.

SAN FEDELE D'INTELVI

Villa Simplicitas €€ *San Fedele d'Intelvi (15 mins' drive from Lake Como), tel: 031 831132, fax: 031 830455, <www.villasimplicitas. it>.* Between lakes Como and Garda, this 19th-century country house enjoys a peaceful rural setting. Downstairs there's a large open fireplace, an antique billiards table, and a conservatory and terrace for meals. Ten characterful guest rooms are decorated with antiques, curios and wrought-iron and brass beds.

VARENNA

Albergo Milano €€ *Via XX Settembre 29, tel: 0341 830298, fax: 0341 830061, <www.varenna.net>.* A gem of a hotel in the centre of picturesque Varenna. There are only eight rooms (book well in advance), all individually furnished in rustic style, with balconies and lake views. The inviting restaurant has a large lakeside terrace for alfresco meals.

LAKE GARDA

GARDONE RIVIERA

Grand Hotel Fasano €€–€€€ *Corso Zanardelli 190, tel: 0365 290220, fax: 0365 290221, <www.grand-hotel-fasano.it>.* A converted 19th-century hunting lodge with extensive and luxuriant gardens and a variety of rooms and views, priced accordingly. The separate Villa Principe on the lake offers water sports, a tennis court and a beach.

Villa Fiordaliso €€€–€€€€ *Corso Zanardelli 132, tel: 0365 20158, fax: 0365 290011, <www.villafiordaliso.it>.* Delightful Art Nouveau villa where Mussolini and Clara Petacci stayed before they were caught and executed in 1945 *(see page 21)*. The hotel is on a busy road but there are gardens leading down to the lake and the Michelin-starred restaurant (one of the best on Garda) has a lakeside terrace. There are just seven rooms: six doubles and the pricey Clara Petacci suite.

GARGNANO

Gardenia al Lago €–€€€ *Via Colletta 53, Villa di Gargnano, tel: 0365 71195, fax: 0365 72594, <www.hotel-dulac.it>.* Delightful villa hotel with gardens down to the lake. The same family have run the hotel for over half a century; guest rooms are traditional with antiques and tiled floors, each with terrace or balcony.

Hotel du Lac €–€€ *Via Colletta 21, Villa di Gargnano, tel: 0365 71107, fax: 0365 71055, <www.hotel-dulac.it>.* Sister hotel of the Gardenia *(see above),*with the same lovely views and family-run atmosphere. Charmingly old fashioned, with handsome antiques in bedrooms; the restaurant overlooks on the lake.

RIVA DEL GARDA

Restel de Fer € *Via Restel de Fer 10, tel: 0464 553481, fax: 0464 552798, <www.resteldefer.com>.* The Meneghelli family, who have been here since 1400, run a highly regarded restaurant *(see page 139)* and offer five guest rooms, all with bathrooms. The minimum stay is three days and there are special rates for stays of a week or more.

SIRMIONE

Grifone € *Vicolo Bisse 5, tel: 030 916014, fax: 030 916548.* One of the few cheaper options in Sirmione, and located right by the castle, the Grifone books up fast. The hotel is family-run, with 16 simply furnished lake-view rooms and an alluring restaurant with waterside terrace.

Villa Cortine €€€€ *Via Grotte 6, tel: 030 9905890, fax: 030 916390, <www.hotelvillacortine.com>.* Opulent and exclusive villa, built in 1870, with a 20th-century wing added to convert it into a hotel. Away from the bustling centre of Sirmione, the hotel enjoys an enticing setting within 4.8 hectares (12 acres) of parkland leading down to the lakeshore. Half board is compulsory in season. Facilities include a jetty with boats to hire, heated and outdoor swimming pool and tennis courts; water sports can be arranged.

TORRI DEL BENACO

Gardesana €–€€ *Piazza Calderini 20, tel: 045 7225411, fax: 045 7225771, <www.hotel-gardesana.com>*. Historic hotel with a very congenial atmosphere, an above-average restaurant *(see page 140)* and comfortable, reasonably priced rooms overlooking the harbour and castle. Royalty, politicians and films stars have stayed here, among them Churchill, Vivien Leigh, Lawrence Olivier and Maria Callas. Minimum three-night stay.

LAKE ORTA

ORTA SAN GUILIO

Orta € *Piazza Motta 1, tel: 0322 90253, fax: 0322 905646, <www. hotelorta.it>*. Old-fashioned hotel which has been taking guests since 1864. It has an enchanting location on the main square, with romantic views of the lake and island. Predictably, the most desirable and expensive of the simple guest rooms are those on the lake side.

Villa Crespi €€€€ *Via Fava 18, tel: 0322 911902, fax: 0322 911919, <www.lagodortahotels.com>*. Opulent Moorish villa dominated by a lofty minaret within parkland near the lake. Charmed by his visit to Baghdad, Cristoforo Benigno Crespi built the villa in 1879. It is now a 4-star hotel, run by a Neapolitan and his wife, offering luxury guest rooms with marble bathrooms (six doubles, eight suites), fitness room, shiatsu, shirò and a Michelin-starred restaurant *(see page 140)*.

PETTENASCO

L'Approdo €€ *Corso Roma 80, Pettenasco, tel: 0323 89345, fax: 0323 89338, <www.lagodortahotels.com>*. On the lakeshore at the small village of Pettenasco, just north of Orta San Giulio, this modern hotel would suit any sports enthusiast. You can windsurf, water-ski, canoe, rent boats, play tennis, swim from the beach or do leisurely lengths in the 25-metre heated outdoor pool. Most of the 73 balconied guest rooms overlook the lake; others look out on to the garden.

CITY HOTELS

BERGAMO

Agnello d'Oro € *Via Gombito 2, tel: 035 249883, <www.agnello doro.it>*. A quaint shuttered building dating from 1600, overlooking a little piazza in the historic upper city. The restaurant, with tables outside by the fountain, has a bistro atmosphere and offers local specialities *(see pages 141–2)*. The 20 guest rooms are fairly basic but all have bath and satellite TV.

VERONA

Aurora €€ *Piazza delle Erbe 2, tel: 045 594717, fax: 045 8010860, <www.hotelaurora.biz>*. Two-star hotel with a homely atmosphere right on the famous Piazza delle Erbe. Guest rooms have recently been refurbished; all have satellite TV and air conditioning, and all but three have bath or shower. A third of the rooms and a second-floor terrace look out on to the square.

Due Torri Hotel Baglioni €€€€ *Piazza Sant'Anastasia 4, tel: 045 595044, fax: 045 8004130, <www.baglionihotels.com>*. Luxury hotel in imposing 14th-century villa, beside the church of Sant'Anastasia. Public rooms are grandiose, with antiques, vaulted ceilings and frescoes. Guest rooms are old-fashioned in style but well-equipped. This is a favourite location of opera stars.

Torcolo € *Vicolo Listone 3, tel: 045 8007512, fax: 045 8004058, <www.hoteltorcolo.it>*. Small, homely and appealing hotel very close to the Arena and popular with opera fans who book their favourite room months in advance of the season. Comfortable guest rooms are individually furnished, all in attractive traditional style. Breakfast can be taken on a small terrace in summer, but since it is not included in the room rate, you may choose instead to have coffee and croissants on Piazza Brà overlooking the Arena.

Recommended Restaurants

The restaurants recommended below range from humble cafés to temples of gastronomy. The list is just a short selection – there are numerous other restaurants in the region which are appealing for their setting, cuisine and service.

It is advisable to make a reservation in high season, especially for a table on a lakeside terrace. Normal opening times are lunch *(pranzo)* noon/12.30pm–2/3pm, and the evening meal *(cena)* 7.30/8pm–10pm or even later in main resorts. Menus at lunch time are frequently cheaper than those offered in the evening. Restaurant bills will usually include €1–€4 per person for bread and cover charge *(pane e coperto)* and sometimes a 10–15 percent service charge. If service is not included it is normal to leave a tip.

The prices indicated are a basic guide for a three-course evening meal per person, including cover charge and service but excluding wine.

€€€€	over 50 euros
€€€	35–50 euros
€€	25–35 euros
€	below 25 euros

LAKE MAGGIORE

BORROMEO ISLANDS

Belvedere € *Via di Mezzo, Isola dei Pescatori, tel: 0323 32292, <www.belvedere-isolapescatori.it>*. An idyllic waterside setting on the charming Isola dei Pescatori, with meals served in the garden, on the verandah or in the lakeview dining room. The restaurant specialises in fresh lake fish such as *laverello* grilled with butter and sage, trout, perch or mixed grill from the lake. By day you get here by ferry, by night the hotel boat will come and collect you from Stresa, Baveno or Pallanza. (Reservations essential for evening meals).

If you're tempted to stay, the Belvedere is also a hotel, with attractive, simply furnished lakeview rooms.

CANNOBIO

Lo Scalo €€€€ *Piazza Vittorio Emanuele III, tel: 0323 71480.* Right on the waterfront in a porticoed 14th-century *palazzo* which once sheltered local fishing boats. Exceptional Piedmontese cuisine, with delicious home-made pastas, fish from the lake and a serious wine list. Closed Mon, Tues lunch.

Sant'Anna €€ *Via Sant'Anna, 30 (on the road to Valle Cannobina), tel: 0323 70682, <www.ristorantesantanna>.* Perched on the edge of the Orrido di Sant'Anna, a spectacular gorge, with a large garden and river-view terrace. The simple menu offers lake and sea fish, delicious pasta and risotto and home-made dessert. Closed Mon.

MERGOZZO

Piccolo Lago €€€€ *Via Filippo Turati 87, Fondotoce, Lake Mergozzo, tel: 0323 586192, <www.piccololago.it>.* The 'Little Lake' restaurant lies on the tiny Lago di Mergozzo, between Mergozzo and Fondotoce. One of the best restaurants in the region, it boasts a beautiful lakeside setting and Michelin-starred cuisine. Traditional Piedmontese dishes, rich risottos and trout, pike and perch from the lake are elegantly prepared and presented. This is also a hotel with 12 modern rooms and lakeside pool. Closed Mon and Jan.

PALLANZA

Albergo Milano €€€€ *Corso Zanitello 2/4, tel: 0323 556816.* Frighteningly pricey but worth splashing out for the great lakeside location by the picturesque old harbour, the exquisite fish dishes and the succulent meat from Piedmont. Needless to say, everything here is freshly sourced, the setting is elegant and the service faultless. Closed Mon dinner and Tues.

STRESA

La Botte € *Via Mazzini 6/8, tel: 0323 30462*. 'The Barrel' is a simple little wood-panelled eatery serving good Piedmontese dishes, hearty steaks as well as pasta and pizzas. Inside tables only. Closed Thurs.

Osteria degli Amici €–€€ *Via A.M. Bolongaro 31, tel: 0323 30453*. Cosy interior and a handful of tables outside under the vines. Popular for pizzas cooked in a wood-fired oven, piscine pastas and risottos, steak or grilled fish. Closed Wed.

LAKE COMO

BELLAGIO

Barchetta €€€ *Salita Mella 18, tel: 031 951389, <www.acena.it/la barchettadibellagio>*. A long-established and consistently good trattoria up a stepped alley from the waterfront. The menu features creative pastas, creamy risottos and delicious fresh fish. A heated terrace means you can enjoy the views even on cool days. Closed Tues.

Silvio €€ *Via Carcano 12, tel: 031 950322*. Above the gardens of Villa Melzi, on the main Bellagio to Como road, this is worth the detour for the freshest of fish, caught by Silvio's family, and the peaceful setting above the lake. *Taglioni al lavarello* (pasta with lake fish) and *semifreddo di grappa e uvetta* (ice cream with grappa and raisins) are house specialities. This is also a hotel with modestly priced rooms.

COMO

Riva €–€€ *Via Cairoli 10, tel: 031 264325*. Choose from around 70 pizzas, a range of imaginative salads or grilled steak or chops with chips and Mediterranean vegetables.

Sociale € *Via Maestri Comacini 8, tel: 031 264042*. There is nothing special gastronomically about the Sociale, but it's very central, right next to the Duomo, and good value for simple meals. Living up to its name, it's a favourite haunt of the locals for both bar and restaurant.

ISOLA COMACINA

Locanda dell'Isola Comacina €€€€ *Isola Comacina, tel: 0344 55083*, <www.comacina.it/isola/locanda_inn.htm>. A gimmicky rather than a gastronomic experience. You are ferried to the deserted island from Sala Comacina and served a rustic lunch of grilled trout and chicken. The meal ends with a rite-of-fire to exorcise the curse put on the island in the 12th century by the Bishop of Como. Closed Tues off-season.

VARENNA

Il Cavatappi €–€€ *Via XX Settembre, tel: 0341 815349*. 'The Corkscrew' is a minute eatery on a little alleyway with just five tables. Simple but delicious cuisine, a well-stocked wine cellar and a very cosy atmosphere. Closed Wed.

Vecchia Varenna €€–€€€ *Contrada Scoscesa 10, tel: 0341 830793*. Irresistable waterside setting with lake and mountain views and an excellent choice of fish. You can have it stuffed with vegetables and herbs, on a spit, in fishcakes, baked with olives and capers or flavouring risottos. Carnivores are not ignored – there is braised donkey, stewed rabbit or – for more conventional tastes – steak and pork. Closed Mon, Jan.

LAKE GARDA

DESENZANO DEL GARDA

Caffè Italia €–€€€ *Piazza Malvezzi 19, tel: 030 9141243*. Historic café in the centre where you can grab a quick morning cappuccino and brioche at the bar with the locals, enjoy a light lunch on the terrace or a blow-out seven-course *menu degustazione* (tasting menu). The piles of prawns, oysters, scallops and other seafood sitting on ice are more than likely to tempt you. Closed Mon.

Esplanade €€€€ *Via Lario 10, tel: 030 9143361.* One of Lake Garda's top restaurants, serving creative modern cuisine in an elegant, formal setting. Among the specialities are eel rolls with pickled vegetables, seafood lasagne and duck ravioli with rosemary and goose liver. Closed Wed.

GARGNANO

La Tortuga di Orietta €€€€ *Via XXIV Maggio 5, tel: 0365 71251.* Save this one for a special occasion and since it's very small make sure to book a table. In the charming fishing village of Gargnano this rustic restaurant serves exquisite dishes and great wines. Fish predominates but you can also find meat antipasti and main courses such as carpaccio of duck and lamb with rosemary and thyme. Closed Tues.

RIVA DEL GARDA

Ristorante Restel de Fer €€–€€€ *Via Restel de Fer 10, tel: 0464 553481.* Delightful rustic trattoria and inn, run by the Meneghelli family since 1400. Many of the dishes are based on ancient recipes. Try Zisan, small fried lakewater fish with onions, or the salmon trout, marinated in fresh herbs and local olive oil, and then grilled. Wash it all down with Trentino wines from the well-stocked cellar and round off the meal with a grappa.

SIRMIONE

Osteria/Vinoteca/Formaggeria € *Piazzetta Mosaici 6, tel: 030 9904432.* A good spot to try out local wines and a platter of local cheeses in the early evening. Many of the wines, including sparkling Prosecco, are sold by the glass.

Risorgimento €€€ *Piazza Carducci 5–6, tel: 030 916325.* Sirmione is packed with takeaway pizza places but for proper food and smart service the Risorgimento is the place to go. On a lively piazza where the ferries come and go, it has a wide choice of fish, served with pasta and risotto, or simply grilled, as well as flambéed steaks and mouthwatering desserts.

TORRI DEL BENACO

Ristorante del Buonricordo, Gardesana Hotel €€€ *Piazza Calderini 20, tel: 045 7225411, <www.hotel-gardesana.com>*. The terrace of this historic hotel *(see page 133)* is a romantic spot overlooking the harbour and castle; and the cuisine is among the best on the lake. Choose from the Lake, Gourmet or Seasonal Menu, or try out specialities such as *la girella di cavedano al burro e timo* (crepes stuffed with chub butter and thyme) or *filetto di lavarello in agrodolce*, flavoursome lake fish cooked in a sweet-and-sour sauce, or the wonderful fish soup. Dinner only.

LAKE ORTA

ORTA SAN GIULIO

Taverna Antico Agnello €€ *Via Olina 18, tel: 0322 90259.* Charming rustic trattoria with emphasis on meat dishes (horse and donkey among them) and specialities from Piedmont. Closed Tues.

Villa Crespi €€€€ *Via G. Fava 8/10, Orta San Giulio, tel: 0322 911902* An exclusive Moorish villa hotel *(see page 133)* with a Neapolitan chef who sources the finest ingredients: mozzarella from southern Italy, shrimps from San Remo, truffles from Alba, locally grown fresh fruit and vegetables. His creative dishes – many of which are Mediterranean – have earned the restaurant a Michelin star. Feast on Sicilian scampi in Martini sauce, ravioli with clams and caviar, lamb stuffed with raisins and pine nuts with black truffle – washed down with wine from the 83-page wine list. Closed Tues, Wed lunch.

CITIES

BERGAMO

Agnello d'Oro €€ *Via Gombito 22, tel: 035 249883.* Atmospheric hotel restaurant in the old upper city serving traditional local dishes with classic polenta or polenta *taragna* (with butter and cheese). In summer you can sit out on the little piazza by the 16th-century fountain. Closed Mon and Sun pm.

Colleoni & dell'Angelo €€€ *Piazza Vecchia 7, Città Alta, tel: 035 232596,* <www.colleonidellangelo.com>. Elegant palace setting with a much sought-after terrace on the stunning central square of the upper city. Exquisite pasta dishes on offer include Bergamo's *casoncelli*, ravioli with sage, butter and almonds, linguine with sea urchins, Beluga caviar, ravioli stuffed with pigeon breast and foie gras with pistaccio. These can be followed by sea bass or gilthead in a sea-salt crust or rack of lamb in a black truffle crust. Closed Mon and two weeks August

Da Mimmo €€–€€€ *Via Colleoni, Città Alta, tel: 035 218535,* <www.ristorantemimmo.com>. In the same family for half a century, Da Mimmo sources the finest raw materials from Bergamo's market and serves strictly traditional regional fare: home-made Bergamasche pastas, outstanding fish dishes, rabbit and polenta, ageing *bagoss* cheese, bread cooked in wood ovens and home-made desserts. You can dine within the 14th-century *palazzo* or in the garden on summer evenings. It's a favourite haunt of locals so reservations (which can be done online) are advisable.

Vineria Cozzi €–€€ *Via Colleoni 22a, tel: 035 238836,* <www.vineriacozzi.it>. Inviting *bottega* popular for its huge choice of Italian wines and varied menu offering *antipasti*, vegetarian dishes such as polenta and *porcini* mushrooms, a selection of cold meats or cheeses and some delicious pastas. The *menu degustazione*, comprising four courses plus a decent glass of wine, is an affordable way of trying several of the specialities. Closed Wed.

BRESCIA

Caffè Floriam €€ *Via Gasparo da Salò 3, tel: 030 41314,* <www.caffefloriamrestaurant.it>. In the heart of the historic centre near Piazza della Loggia, this is a long-established, welcoming café/restaurant serving traditional home-cooked dishes. Closed Tues.

VARESE

Ristorante Bologna €–€€ *Via Broggi 7, Varese, tel: 0332 232100.*
A hotel restaurant offering good-value set menus, featuring fresh
pasta such as *tagliolini alla crema di asparagi* (with cream of asparagus), *gnocchi con salsa gialla di noce e zafferano* (with yellow
walnut and saffron sauce), followed by meat or fish, and one of the
creamy, calorific home-made desserts. Coffee and a *digestivo* are
thrown in too.

Vecchia Riva €€–€€€ *Via Macchi 146, Schiranna, Varese, tel:
0332 329300, <www.vecchiariva.com>.* Set on the banks of the unspoilt Lake Varese, Vecchia Riva has a sheltered garden and serves
good fish, risotto and pasta dishes. The restaurant is attached to a
small two-star hotel that offers functional modern rooms.

VERONA

12 Apostoli €€€€ *Vicolo Corticella San Marco 3, tel: 045 596999,
<www.12apostoli.it>.* Charming, traditional restaurant in an 18th
century *palazzo*, with frescoed vaulted ceilings and classic cuisine.
It is named after 12 friends who used to do business here in the mid
18th century over a simple dish of pasta or beans and a glass of
wine. Closed Mon and Sun dinner.

Brek € *Piazza Brà 20, tel: 045 8004561, <www.brek.it>.* Italian
chain, where you help yourself to simple pastas, soup, fresh vegetables, salads, meat dishes and desserts. Excellent value and a perfect
spot on the Listone, overlooking the Arena.

Giovanni Rana Tre Corone €€€€ *Piazza Brà 16, tel: 045
8002462, <www.trattoriagiovannirana.it>.* Prime location in an historic palace overlooking the Arena. You can choose from the *Menu
Tradizionale*, or, in July and August, a pre-opera (6.30–9pm) or post-
opera (midnight–2.30am) menu. The varied à la carte menu features
home-made pastas, salt cod with polenta, steak tartare, saddle of
venison, horse stew, veal fillet and typical Venetian dishes such as
sarde in saor. Closed Mon and Sun dinner except July and August.

INDEX